SPECIAL EDUCATIONAL NEEDS

A Parent's Guide

Need
— 2 —
Know

Antonia Chitty
& Victoria
Dawson

D0193261

First published in Great Britain in 2008 by
Need2Know
Remus House
Coltsfoot Drive
Peterborough
PE2 9JX
Telephone 01733 898103
Fax 01733 313524
www.need2knowbooks.co.uk

Second Edition 2010

Need2Know is an imprint of Forward Press Ltd.
www.forwardpress.co.uk
All Rights Reserved
© Antonia Chitty & Victoria Dawson 2008
SB ISBN 978-1-86144-116-4
Cover photograph: Dreamstime

Contents

Introduction 5

Chapter 1   Your Child's Speech 9

Chapter 2   Global Developmental Delay 19

Chapter 3   Autistic Spectrum Disorder 29

Chapter 4   Your Child's Hearing and Sight 37

Chapter 5   Physical Disabilities 49

Chapter 6   Hereditary and Genetic Conditions 57

Chapter 7   Specific Learning Difficulties 63

Chapter 8   Family Life 73

Chapter 9   Behaviour Difficulties at Home 81

Chapter 10   Sleep Issues 91

Chapter 11   Education 101

Chapter 12   Housing and Finance 109

Help List 115

Introduction

Do you worry about your child's development? Maybe you know that your child has special educational needs. Or perhaps you work with children and want to know more about special educational needs? Whatever your situation, this book will guide you through the confusing diagnoses and complex systems you might meet.

If you're confused by the terms, read this quick guide:

Special educational needs (SEN): learning difficulties, developmental or physical disabilities or mental health problems can mean that a child may need extra or different help to other children of the same age.

Disability: children may be born with or develop a physical impairment, sensory impairment or problems with learning and understanding. Because of the way that the world works, they may be seen as disabled.

Additional needs: a disability or learning difficulty requiring extra support.

Different types of additional need

The first half of the book looks at the different types of additional need. Poor or delayed speech is one of the most common signs that parents pick up on. If you are concerned about your pre-schooler's language, have a word with your health visitor. Read chapter 1 to find more about speech problems and how to help your child.

Chapter 2 can help you find out more if your child:

- Has poor co-ordination.
- Struggles with talking.
- Has a short attention span.
- Appears socially immature.

You can read about developing your child's movement and play skills, speech and social communication.

Chapter 3 explains about a group of conditions called autistic spectrum disorder (ASD). If your child has problems understanding other people's feelings and expressing their own, they may be on the autistic spectrum. There are different levels of impairment, so some children can have limited speech while others have good language skills.

It is vital to get your child's eyes and ears checked or they may struggle unnecessarily. Chapter 4 will help you make sure your child is seeing and hearing as well as possible, and also tells you about how to get help if your child has a serious impairment.

Alongside special educational needs, some children have accompanying physical impairments which chapter 5 examines. Chapter 6 looks at conditions that may run in the family or be inherited, and chapter 7 fills you in on specific learning difficulties (SpLDs), including dyslexia, dysgraphia and dyscalculia, and how they link to dyspraxia.

Help for you

It can be bewildering when your child needs extra help. There are plenty of different professionals out there, but who can help with your particular problem? This book will help you find:

- The right person to call.

- The quickest way to get a referral.

- How to get through the system.

The second half of the book is your guide to making day-to-day life easier. You will find contacts for charities and organisations, and will discover what you are entitled to in the way of local authority (LA) resources and how to access them. This part of the book also looks at how to get the emotional support you and your family need, especially chapter 8.

Chapter 9 gives you practical tips to handle behaviour difficulties from experts who are working with children with special needs. Chapter 10 deals with sleep. Many parents of children with special needs deal with disturbed sleep long after they expected sleep problems to be over. Sleep deprivation impacts on the whole family, and for the child who is getting poor sleep every night it makes it harder to concentrate and learn. If you are at the end of your tether and would do anything for an unbroken night then read this chapter.

Getting it right at school can be a battle. This book will tell you what support is available and how to access it. From the early years, before your child starts school, there is additional help for children with special educational needs. Read chapter 11 for the low down on education, special schools and educating your child in the mainstream state system.

And finally, you may find that you need to pay for adaptations for your home or extra transport. Perhaps you have given up income to be at home to help your child more. The last chapter of the book, chapter 12, looks at the practical issues of housing and finance, with tips from other parents and information about benefits.

Although this book refers to children as 'your child', it is also an essential guide if you work with children or have a friend or relative with special educational needs. Look at the help list at the back of the book for contact details of any organisations mentioned.

Disclaimer

This book is for general information about special educational needs only. Anyone with health concerns should consult their GP or healthcare professional in the first instance. This book can be used alongside professional medical advice but does not replace it – always check with your GP or healthcare professional in the first instance.

Chapter One

Your Child's Speech

Poor language or delayed speech can be one of the first signs that your child may have special needs. Speech or language impairment can occur by itself, but may be a sign of hearing loss, autism, learning disabilities or a range of other additional needs. Read on if you are worried about your child's speech.

Signs that there may be a problem

Children develop at different rates; around 6 in every 100 children have a speech, language or communication problem at some point, rising to 1 in 10 children who have other difficulties. If you think your child may have speech problems, check the list of signs below, based on information from the speech and communication charity Afasic (www.afasic.org.uk).

Tick if your child shows these signs:

Under 1

☐ Lack of eye contact.

☐ Little or no babbling.

☐ No response to noise.

Age 1-2 years

☐ Little or no speech.

☐ Lack of understanding.

☐ Poor listening.

☐ Seeming not to hear or pay attention.

- ☐ Lack of normal play for age.

Age 2-3 years

- ☐ Cannot say any words.
- ☐ Does not listen or respond to simple instructions.
- ☐ Makes little or no eye contact.
- ☐ Difficult to draw their attention to things.
- ☐ Frustration or tantrums.
- ☐ Very shy.

Age 3-5

- ☐ Finds it hard to produce many sounds.
- ☐ Only parents or close family can understand what they say.
- ☐ Muddles speech or uses words in the wrong order.
- ☐ Struggles to learn new words.
- ☐ Misses out words in a sentence.
- ☐ Finds it hard to link words together.
- ☐ Forgets instructions or a conversation almost as soon as they are said.
- ☐ Finds it difficult to pay attention to instructions or a conversation.
- ☐ Makes inappropriate answers or comments.
- ☐ Does not understand how to take turns in a conversation.
- ☐ Speaking and playing skills are far behind.
- ☐ Lack of understanding of turn-taking.
- ☐ Poor rhyming skills.
- ☐ Co-ordination difficulties.

5 years and upwards

- [ ] Learning difficulties in classroom.
- [ ] Poor social skills, few friends.
- [ ] Emotional and behavioural difficulties.
- [ ] Difficulties with word games.
- [ ] Jumps inappropriately from one topic to another in conversation.
- [ ] Finds it difficult to switch topics.
- [ ] Finds it hard to learn to read.
- [ ] Struggles to understand abstract ideas such as time or emotions.
- [ ] Misinterprets language which isn't literal – like 'pull your socks up'.

Why not to worry

Children are different. Some say their first word before they are one, while others utter few words in their second year but catch up before they are three. It is normal for children to muddle or mispronounce words. Your child can have delayed speech if your family is bilingual or if they are the youngest in a large family and older siblings rarely let them get a word in. Look at how other children of the same age are developing and talk to your health visitor if you are concerned.

Getting your child's speech checked

Picking up your child's problem at an early stage will get them the help they need. Kate Freeman, professional adviser at I CAN, says: 'There is likely to be a wait for an appointment, so take action as soon as you suspect there might be a problem'. Poor speech may be a sign of hearing problems, so it's important to get help. See chapter 4 for more about getting your child's hearing checked.

Getting a referral

You can contact an NHS speech and language therapist (SLT) without a referral from your GP. Ask your local NHS trust for details of who to contact or look at the list of SLT departments on I CAN's Talking Point website. (I CAN works to support the development of speech, language and communication skills in all children, with a special focus on those who find this hard: children with speech, language and communication needs). If you're unsure of where to go or want your child's hearing checked too, ask your GP or health visitor. Your child's school can also refer your child for speech and language therapy, and some schools have an SLT who visits regularly.

What happens next?

You will be given an appointment for an initial assessment, which should be within about six weeks of your call. Waiting time varies between areas and you can wait up to a year. In some localities, assessments are one-to-one, but in others an SLT may assess a group of children.

When you visit an SLT, they will assess your child's speech – how they make speech sounds, the words that they use and their level of understanding. They will check this in relation to your child's age and general development, and will look at how your child plays and communicates with others. The SLT can refer your child to a paediatrician if they feel their difficulties go beyond speech.

The SLT will ask about:

- Your child's birth.
- When they learnt to sit, stand, walk and reached other developmental milestones.
- Any difficulties with feeding (which uses the same muscles as speech).
- Use of dummies.
- Your child's health.
- Any speech, language or communication problems in the family.

Make notes about your own child's history:

Your child's birth..

....

....

When your child learnt to sit, walk and stand ....

....

....

Your child's feeding ....

....

....

Your child's use of dummies ....

....

....

Your child's health ....

....

....

Your child's speech ....

....

....

The SLT will observe your child and interact with them as they play games. They will need to work out whether, for example, your child can play tea parties with a teddy and understand that a teddy can represent a person. If your child is able to do this, the SLT will make a more formal assessment, asking them to look at pictures or follow instructions. For example, your child may be shown a broom, a cup and a car and then asked which one they would sweep the floor with. Don't try to help your child at this point – the SLT will be using standard questions to see how your child responds in comparison to other children of a similar age. There are not always right and wrong answers: it is not an exam.

If your child is struggling, the SLT will take a break or stop. The SLT is trained to get the best from your child and sometimes may suggest you come back to finish the assessment.

At the end of the assessment, the SLT will give you an initial diagnosis and will explain whether your child needs help with the following:

- Developing a better understanding of words.
- Making speech sounds.
- The words your child is using.

You should also get a written report in the post.

Speech and language therapy

The SLT often suggests activities for you and your child to do at home. These activities can help to stimulate your child's speech and language development. You may be asked to:

- Read to your child.
- Speak in short sentences using simple words.
- Repeat what your child says, using correct grammar and pronunciation.
- Play word games.

Your SLT may ask you to bring your child in regularly once a week or once a month to develop skills that are necessary for good speech, language and communication development. The SLT may also liaise with your child's school so that work can be continued in class.

Sessions may be individual or in a group of children working on similar issues. Once they begin, a group may meet for six weeks, followed by a break to allow your child to consolidate the skills they have learnt. However, due to waiting lists, there may be a delay before sessions start.

Remember though, the work you do with your child at home is almost more important than the sessions with the SLT because you spend so much more time with your child.

Who can help?

Speech and language therapist (SLT): a health professional trained to diagnose, assess and treat adults and children with language, speech, voice, communication or swallowing disorders which affect their ability to communicate. Most work in the NHS, some offer private appointments and some work in schools.

You can find independent SLTs through ASLTIP, the Association of Speech and Language Therapists in Independent Practice. A private assessment will cost in the region of £80-90 and a private follow up around £60-70, depending on your area.

You may also get help from a special educational needs co-ordinator (SENCO) (see chapter 11) or an educational psychologist (see chapter 7).

Causes of speech and language problems

Children can have different sorts of speech and language problems, and some may have difficulties understanding the meaning of sentences or words. It can be especially hard for these children to grasp words that are about abstract ideas, such as 'sad', or they may take phrases too literally. Other children have problems understanding how we use language socially. They may not know when it is their turn to talk and may interrupt or talk about topics which do not seem to fit the conversation. Some children have problems using language, while others have difficulties with understanding too. Difficulties can be mild and dealt with by speech and language therapy, or more severe and long term.

Problems in this area can occur without any other difficulties or as part of a range of conditions or a syndrome like Asperger's. A speech and language delay may be a sign of global developmental delay (see chapter 2), hearing problems or frequent ear infections. Some children may also have a problem with their mouth, tongue, nose or breathing.

'Your SLT may ask you to bring your child in regularly once a week or once a month to develop skills that are necessary for good speech, language and communication development.'

More help

There are ways to help children with severe difficulties in speaking or understanding. Sometimes it is recommended that you use signing systems such as Makaton to help develop your child's language skills. If there are significant difficulties with a child's ability to make themselves understood, they may benefit from electronic voice output devices and adapted computers. The NHS speech and language therapy service or your LA can supply these.

Talk to the SLT about help for your child at school and beyond. All schools and pre-school settings must have a named person who co-ordinates additional support to children (the special educational needs co-ordinator or SENCO). Talking to your child's SENCO will help identify the level of support they need in school. You can also ask if a Statement of Special Educational Needs would assist in getting your child the help they need.

'Talking to your child's SENCO will help identify the level of support they need in school. You can also ask if a Statement of Special Educational Needs would assist in getting your child the help they need.'

Need2Know

Summing Up

A speech, language or understanding problem may be the first sign that your child has special educational needs. There is a lot that you can do to help your child develop their speech, language and understanding. Get some help from an SLT and you can help your child to make progress. The main thing to do is talk to your child, using simple, clear words. Here is a quick checklist so you can check what action to try next:

☐ Spend time every day playing with your child. While you play, talk about what they are doing using two or three word sentences.

☐ Set up everyday situations, like shopping or meal times, using toys to help your child practise useful words. Have a box of objects you can use and play with, such as a hairbrush and comb, or use pictures to talk about parts of the body.

☐ Play games that involve putting a toy on, under, in front of or behind something and repeat phrases like, 'Where's teddy?'

☐ Sing songs, say rhymes and read simple books that repeat words.

☐ Ask your child open questions or encourage them to make a choice, e.g. between juice or milk.

Chapter Two

Global
Developmental Delay

Childhood can be broken down into many developmental stages, like crawling, moving onto solids and speaking a first word. A developmental delay means that some of these milestones have not been achieved at the expected stage in your child's life. This chapter looks at the areas of development that may be delayed, how your child is assessed, the professionals that you may meet and how to support your child's development.

What is developmental delay?

You may hear professionals talking about developmental delay, which simply means that your child has not reached a particular milestone at the stage in their life that would be expected. For example, if your child is late to walk, they may be described as having a developmental delay.

Areas that children may be developmentally delayed in can include:

- Physical and gross motor skills – how your child moves their arms, legs and body.

- Fine motor skills – how they make the small movements needed to hold a pen or pick up a bead.

- Communication and language – how your child talks and understands.

- Social interaction – how your child relates to others.

- Cognitive – how your child thinks and learns.

- Emotional – how your child behaves.

Each one of these will be explained in detail further on in this chapter. Global developmental delay simply means that your child is delayed in two or more of these areas.

Why is my child delayed?

There are many reasons why your child may be developmentally delayed. Sometimes it can simply be a lack of experience; for example, if they haven't played with other children because they are an only child, they may be delayed in their social interactions. Alternatively, the delay could be due to something that occurred while your child was in the womb, such as exposure to infection. Premature babies are at more risk of being developmentally delayed than other children, and it can also run in the family.

Getting your child assessed

As a parent, you know your child better than anyone else. All children develop at different rates, so try not to make comparisons between your child and your friend's children. If you are worried that your child's development is delayed, talk to your health visitor or, if your child is over five, see their class teacher or GP.

Before you go to the appointment, make sure you list your concerns. Explain why you think they are delayed in this area. For example, if you are worried about their language, write down words that they use, any sounds that you hear and the number of words that they can say. Having this information in front of you will keep you focused and will ensure that you cover everything you want to talk about during the appointment.

'As a parent, you know your child better than anyone else. All children develop at different rates, so try not to make comparisons between your child and your friend's children.'

Write down any concerns you have about your child's development here:

How your child moves their arms, legs and body ....
....
....

How your child makes small movements ....
....
....

How your child talks and understands ....
....
....

How your child relates to others ....
....
....

How your child thinks and learns ....
....
....

How your child behaves ....
....
....

If the professional thinks that your child may have developmental delay, they can refer you to a local assessment centre where your child will be assessed by a range of therapists. You will find out if your child is delayed and will get advice about how to help them develop. If the professional does not see any cause for concern, you can ask for a second opinion from another healthcare professional.

Gross motor skills

You might hear professionals talking about 'gross motor skills'. This is the skill that your child uses to move the large muscles in their body: their legs, arms and torso. Walking, crawling, climbing and jumping are all based on your child's gross motor skills. If your child has a delay in this area, they may not be able to do physical tasks as well as expected for their age.

A physiotherapist may assess your child to see if their gross motor skills are delayed. If necessary, they may ask to see your child regularly to offer them a personalised therapy programme or they may show you exercises to perform with your child at home. Ask the therapist if there is anything that you can do to help your child's physical development.

The physiotherapist will ask you questions about your child and when they learnt to sit up, crawl and walk with furniture. Think about these and make notes to take to the assessment.

'The physiotherapist will ask you questions about your child and when they learnt to sit up, crawl and walk with furniture. Think about these and make notes to take to the assessment.'

At what age did your child first:

Sit up? ....

Crawl? ....

Walk with support, e.g. from furniture? ....

Fine motor skills

Fine motor skills are the small movements that children need to master in order to do things like hold a pencil well or play a musical instrument.

An occupational therapist (OT) can check your child's fine motor skills as well as how they make sense of visual information. The therapist will support your child to be independent and can aid with self-help skills such as finding cutlery so that your child can feed themselves or providing toileting aids to promote their independence. Ask if there are any activities you can do at home to develop your child's fine motor skills and find out if your child may benefit from specialist equipment for school. The occupational therapist can also send activities to your child's school, if appropriate.

Communication and language delay

If your child is late to speak, it is hard to determine whether they have just a delay or a speech and language disorder. If you are concerned about their speech, ask your GP for a referral to an SLT or contact the department direct (see chapter 1). Your GP may want to check your child's hearing to make sure that hearing problems aren't affecting their language development. Chapter 4 discusses hearing tests in depth.

If your child is assessed by an SLT, be sure to tell them all the things that your child can do. Make a list of words that your child uses and note whether your child can put two or three words together.

Words my child uses: ....
....
....
....

They may ask you about your child's understanding of language, so you need to work out whether you need to point to make your child understand or if they understand without prompting when you ask them, for example, to 'go and wash your hands'. Mention any concerns about your child's feeding or drinking too and ask if there is anything you can do at home to encourage language development.

Social interaction

The SLT may also assess your child's social interaction or how your child interacts with others. They will look at whether your child makes eye contact, if they approach other children and how they respond to adults. The SLT may also ask you questions around these areas.

Before the appointment, think about whether you have any worries with how your child interacts with others. Do they have friends to play with? Do they make eye contact when you speak to them? Are they generally sociable or do they tend to be withdrawn?

Write about your child here:

'If your child is already in school or pre-school, ask the teacher if they are concerned about your child's cognitive ability and what you can do to support your child's learning.'

Do they have friends to play with? ....

Do they make eye contact when you speak to them? ....

Are they sociable or withdrawn? ....

Cognitive delay

Cognitive delay describes a delay in your child's ability to think, learn, process information and problem solve. As a parent, you can encourage development of your child's cognitive ability by:

- Speaking to them.
- Providing a stimulating environment with lots of activities.
- Offering them lots of varied experiences, e.g. by visiting different places.

Pre-school can help children to develop skills in all areas. If your child is already in school or pre-school, ask the teacher if they are concerned about your child's cognitive ability and what you can do to support your child's learning.

Emotional delay

A health professional can observe your child and ask questions to see if there are any concerns about their emotional development and how they behave. You may be asked whether they have more tantrums than expected for their age. Do they have irrational fears? How is their sleep pattern? Do they find it difficult to separate from their main carer? It is important that any such difficulties are recognised and addressed early so that you can work with the right professionals to help your child. Behaviour difficulties are dealt with in depth in chapter 9.

Write about your child here:

Do they have more tantrums than expected for their age? ....

Do they have irrational fears? ....

How is their sleep pattern? ....

Do they find it difficult to separate from their main carer? ....

Early intervention

Early intervention is important if your child is showing delayed development. A child generally develops skills in a set order, for example they need to learn to sit before they can walk. So the sooner any issue is addressed, the less impact it will have on other areas of development.

Getting help from the right therapists as soon as possible can put your mind at rest; it's reassuring to know that an expert is on hand to answer your questions and guide you through the process. It is better for your child's self-esteem to get difficulties addressed as soon as possible. Their confidence will also be boosted by working with therapists who can set them small, achievable targets.

'Getting help from the right therapists as soon as possible can put your mind at rest; it's reassuring to know that an expert is on hand to answer your questions and guide you through the process.'

Making life easier

If you are told your child has global developmental delay, tell the school or pre-school. If you are having difficulties at home as a direct result of your child's delay, speak to the appropriate therapist and ask them for suggestions to resolve these problems. These may range from behaviour difficulties to safety issues in the home – so you will need to get help.

Sometimes it helps to speak to another parent who has a child with the same diagnosis. Making Contact is an organisation that puts parents in touch with each other. Visit their website at www.makingcontact.org.

Summing Up

Global developmental delay means that your child has not reached two or three milestones at the expected age and stage. Therapists can help your child reach their full potential. Ask your GP for a referral if you are not sure how to get help, or refer yourself to some therapists directly. Remember to celebrate all that your child does achieve; development is a journey and not a race.

Here is a quick checklist so you know what action to try next:

- [ ] If you are worried that your child is not meeting their developmental milestones, speak to your GP or health visitor.

- [ ] If your child is assessed, prepare for the assessment by writing down information about each area of their development, what they do well and your concerns.

- [ ] Ask the therapists for advice about supporting your child's development.

- [ ] Speak to other parents and share information.

Chapter Three

Autistic Spectrum Disorder

Approximately 1 in every 100 children have an autistic spectrum disorder. This chapter looks at the signs of autism, what to do if you suspect your child is autistic, how a diagnosis is made and how to get help. You can read about Asperger's syndrome too.

What is autism?

You may hear autism being referred to as an autistic spectrum disorder or an ASD. It is described as being on a 'spectrum' because it affects children in different ways and in varying degrees. It can affect people from any race or class but is found more frequently in boys. Autism is a lifelong disability and a child with autism will grow up to be an adult with autism.

The cause is still being researched and, while there is no 'cure', there are things you can do to help your child learn and develop to the best of their potential.

Signs of autistic spectrum disorder

The three main areas of difficulty affecting all people with autism are known by professionals as the 'triad of impairments'. This is a term that you will hear used if your child is assessed for autism. The 'triad of impairments' means that a child will have difficulty with:

- Verbal and non-verbal language – known as social communication.
- Fitting in – known as social interaction.
- Seeing things from the point of view of others – known as social imagination.

Using the boxes overleaf, tick if your child shows these signs.

Social communication

If your child is autistic they might not understand some of the following:

- [ ] Facial expressions: a frown to indicate a warning may not be noticed.
- [ ] Tone of voice.
- [ ] Jokes and sarcasm.
- [ ] Common phrases and sayings: asking a child to 'jump in the bath' may be taken literally.
- [ ] Rules of conversation: they may speak about their own interests at length and not take into account the need of the listener. A child with autism may echo things that have just been said by another person, known as 'echolalia'.
- [ ] Using language appropriately: speech is often delayed and may be unusual in its tone and pattern.
- [ ] Some children with autism may have limited speech and communicate with sign language or visual symbols.

Difficulty with social interaction

Children with autism find it difficult to understand emotions and feelings, making it difficult for them to fit in socially. They may:

- [ ] Not understand unwritten social rules: they may comment on somebody being overweight and not realise that this is inappropriate.
- [ ] Avoid eye contact.
- [ ] Seem insensitive because they do not recognise how others are feeling.
- [ ] Prefer to spend time alone rather than playing with other children or adults.
- [ ] Not seek comfort from others.
- [ ] Appear to behave oddly.
- [ ] Find it difficult to form friendships.

Difficulty with social imagination

Social imagination allows us to put ourselves in the position of others and predict how they may feel. Difficulties with social imagination mean that children with autism find it hard to:

- [ ] Understand and interpret other people's thoughts, feelings and actions.
- [ ] Predict what may happen next in a situation.
- [ ] Understand the concept of danger.
- [ ] Play in an imaginative way: instead, they may stick to favourite toys and perform the same actions repeatedly.
- [ ] Accept a change in routine.
- [ ] Cope in new or unfamiliar situations.

Other related characteristics

Tick if your child shows these signs:

- [ ] Rules can be important to children with autism. They may stick to rules rigidly and try to ensure that everybody else follows the rules too.
- [ ] Some children can find noise physically painful while other children may not feel pain or extreme temperature. Some children may flap their hands or rock and others may cover their ears or eyes.
- [ ] Intense special interests are common and can be anything ranging from trains to music.
- [ ] Children with autism may also have learning difficulties. Other conditions are also associated with autism such as ADHD, dyslexia and dyspraxia.
- [ ] Children on the autistic spectrum can self harm or show other inappropriate behaviour.

Why diagnose autism?

A diagnosis can help your child and your family understand about areas of difficulty, and gives you access to support services. If you are worried that your child may have autism, ask your GP or health visitor if your child can be referred for assessment. You can also ask at your child's school or pre-school if they have the same difficulties there. Children can be diagnosed with autism from around the age of two years.

Assessment for autism

There is no simple test to diagnose autism, and assessment varies across the UK. Usually professionals will be involved from health and education. Professionals that you may meet can include:

'Children can be diagnosed with autism from around the age of two.'

- Paediatrician: a doctor specialising in children.
- Speech and language therapist (SLT): (see chapter 1).
- Occupational therapist (OT): (see chapters 2 and 5).
- Specialist teacher: an expert in special educational needs and teaching children with autism.
- Physiotherapist: (see chapters 2 and 5).
- Clinical psychologist: someone who works with children and their families to reduce psychological distress.
- Educational psychologist: (see chapter 7).

You, as parents, have an important role in gathering information to support the diagnosis, so you will need to tell the professionals about your child's history. You might be asked about this via a questionnaire or during an interview with a professional.

The team assessing your child may also:

- Observe your child at home and school.
- Gather information from other professionals such as school teachers.
- Look at your child's work. Drawings may be used for younger children.

Your child may also be given other specific tests – ask the professionals involved in assessing your child what the procedure will be.

The diagnostic process is a complex one. Once the information is collected it will be analysed in detail, which could take several months. You should then get a jargon free report that is positive in its tone.

Receiving your child's diagnosis

No matter how prepared you feel, receiving news that your child has autism can be devastating and you may not feel able to take in all the information that is given to you.

You will usually be given some written information about autism, but when you read this, remember that your child may not show all of the behaviours that are described. Read the material selectively and pick out the bits that relate to your child.

Sometimes the amount of information is overwhelming, so don't feel that you have to read everything. If you want someone to explain the information to you then call the National Autistic Society helpline (see help list) or telephone the professional that made the diagnosis.

Parent training programmes

The National Autistic Society has developed two training programmes for parents following diagnosis.

- The EarlyBird programme – for parents of pre-school children.

- The EarlyBird Plus programme – for parents of children aged four to eight years old.

The EarlyBird programme can help you to understand your child's autism and can make you feel more in control. It looks at how to improve communication between you and your child, how to anticipate challenging behaviour and how to handle it when it happens.

'No matter how prepared you feel, receiving news that your child has autism can be devastating and you may not feel able to take in all the information that is given to you.'

The EarlyBird Plus programme trains parents and a professional who works closely with the child to maximise consistent support for the child. The programme focuses on developing good practice, confidence building and encouraging parents and professionals to work together to problem solve.

The Help! programme provides parents and carers with information and advice after a diagnosis. It also gives helpful support strategies and signposts onto local support services. For further information about any of these courses and to find out if they are available in your area, contact the National Autistic Society helpline (see help list.)

Marie recently attended the EarlyBird programme: 'I'm so glad I signed up for the training. I now feel much more confident when dealing with Dylan's behaviour and I've also realised I'm not alone. I met other parents who are going through a similar thing to our family and I have made some supportive friends.'

Practical tips

Follow these tips to make everyday life easier for you and your child:

- Stick to a routine if possible. Children with autism like to know what is happening when.

- Find a trigger for problem behaviour. Your child may be highly sensitive to a noise and a passing police car siren will disturb them. Once you can identify a trigger, you can try to troubleshoot before it happens again.

- Modify your expectations. A child with autism will need to be set small, achievable targets. If they can't sit down at a table for a full family meal, encourage them to sit down for a couple of minutes initially and build on their success.

- Use clear, simple language. If you tell your child it is 'raining cats and dogs', they will be disappointed to see rain falling from the sky!

- Support their understanding of emotions. When your child smiles, tell them they have a 'happy' face. When they cry, tell them that they are feeling 'sad'.

- If your child has delayed or impaired language, a speech therapist may suggest using a 'Picture Exchange Communication System'(PECS).

Your child selects and gives you a photograph of an everyday item to indicate their need. For example, if they wanted a drink they would select a photograph of the drink and hand it to you.

▪ Invite friends over and support your child by modelling how to play with other children.

▪ Develop good home/school partnerships and tell your child's teacher what works well for you at home. They may be able to use some of the tips in school. You can also use ideas from school so your child is dealt with consistently.

▪ Most importantly, celebrate the achievements that your child does make.

Education and your child

Many autistic children can be educated in mainstream school alongside their peers. If you are concerned about your child's schooling, ask the assessment team if there is a specialist teacher that you can speak to. You can also contact your LA's special educational needs department to find out what specialist provision is available for children with autism in your area. See chapter 11 for further information about education.

If your child attends school or pre-school, talk to the special educational needs co-ordinator (SENCO). They will be able to discuss with you any concerns that you have about education.

Asperger's syndrome

Asperger's is similar to autism, though people with Asperger's have fewer problems with speech. They also have average or above average intelligence and do not have difficulty with learning. They may, however, have what is called a 'specific learning disorder' such as dyslexia or dyspraxia (see chapter 7). They may also have other conditions such as ADHD and epilepsy. Children with Asperger's syndrome can often lead full and independent lives.

Summing Up

Receiving a diagnosis of an ASD can feel devastating, but there are strategies to develop your child's skills. Support groups can be a useful way to find out information. Here is a quick checklist so you can check what action to try next:

☐ If you are worried that your child may have an ASD, talk to your GP, health visitor and the SENCO at school.

☐ At the assessment centre, ask for advice about your child's education and how to support their development at home.

☐ Visit the National Autistic Society's website (www.nas.org.uk).

☐ Look for local support groups.

For more specific information about autism, please see *Autism – A Parent's Guide* (Need2Know).

Chapter Four

Your Child's
Hearing and Sight

If your child has special needs, they have a higher risk of hearing or sight problems. This chapter explains how to get your child's hearing and sight tested. The sooner a problem is spotted, the sooner your child can get the help they need, be it glasses, a hearing aid or equipment to help them at home and at school.

Hearing

Signs of hearing problems

Children with special educational needs have a higher chance of having hearing problems compared to others. This may be temporary, but it is still important to spot it and get your doctor's advice because if it continues it can interfere with your child's social development and learning. Signs of hearing loss in children can easily be mistaken for difficult moods or being distracted, so check if your child:

Tick if your child shows these signs:

☐ Doesn't react when spoken to.

☐ Appears inattentive or prone to daydreaming.

☐ Listens to the TV at high volume.

☐ Talks too loudly.

'Children with special educational needs have a higher chance of having hearing problems compared to others. This may be temporary, but it is still important to spot it and get your doctor's advice because if it continues it can interfere with your child's social development and learning.'

☐ Talks too quietly.

☐ Mispronounces words and doesn't speak clearly.

☐ Says 'what?' very often because they haven't heard what you said.

☐ Becomes unsettled at school.

☐ Is often tired, grumpy, frustrated or over-active.

An undiagnosed hearing problem can slow or stop your child learning language skills, makes communication difficult and can hold back their confidence and social development.

Checking your child's hearing

Visit your GP if you think your child may have a hearing problem. They can check whether there is a problem like a build up of wax; something that can occur more commonly in small ear canals. The GP can arrange for a referral to your local children's audiology service and you will then be sent an appointment for a hearing test. Try to avoid appointments at times of the day when your child is usually tired.

Routine checks

Most children born since 2005 will have had their hearing checked soon after birth in the Newborn Hearing Screening Programme (http://hearing. screening.nhs.uk). Children can still develop hearing problems as they grow. At around two or three years, if your child has a check up with a health visitor, they may ask you questions about hearing. A 'hearing sweep' test may be given by the school nurse when your child starts school. This checks your child's hearing at different pitches.

What the test involves

If your child is referred to an audiology clinic, they will have a range of tests. The professional will look into their ears and then they will ask your child to wear headphones and respond when they hear a sound. Your child may find these requests strange or scary, but you can help by practising 'checking their ears'. If you have a set of headphones, show your child how to wear them and let them try them on several times until they are comfortable with the idea. You could also try playing sounds, for example ask them to put a small toy in a box when they hear a sound. This is the sort of thing they may be asked to do at the test, so it's good preparation.

More tests

If a test shows that your child's hearing might not be 100%, you will be asked to bring them in for more tests. If the test shows the same result, you may see an ear, nose and throat specialist doctor (ENT) who will talk about how to help your child. Ask about the cause of your child's hearing loss, as this will affect what happens next.

- Sometimes you may be offered medical treatment for ear infections or minor surgery for a condition like 'glue ear', where the middle ear has become inflamed and sticky fluid builds up behind the eardrum. This is quite common in young children and often gets better on its own, but if it continues it may need to be treated.

- Your child may be offered hearing aids (see overleaf). These days, children who are born with a permanent hearing problem are usually identified in the first few months of life through newborn screening and further tests.

- If your child is found to be profoundly deaf, cochlear implants may be an option. The audiology staff will discuss the details of this with you.

> ## Who can help?
>
> Audiologist: an audiologist identifies and assesses hearing problems, and can recommend or provide ways to help and refer you to other specialist services.
>
> Your child may also see a doctor, a specialist teacher (see chapter 3) or an SLT. (see chapter 1).

Causes of hearing loss

Some children are born with hearing difficulties which often have a genetic cause even if there is no apparent deafness in the family. Hearing problems can also result from difficulties during or before birth, which have effects on the baby. Hearing loss during childhood can be caused by head injuries or illnesses like meningitis, mumps or measles. Ear infections and 'glue ear' can cause temporary hearing loss and, if they do not clear up, may lead to long-term problems. Children sometimes poke things into their ears which can block the ear or damage the eardrum.

Getting a hearing aid

Modern digital hearing aids are helpful and will be programmed by your audiologist to suit your child's hearing loss. This will make it much easier for them to hear sounds and follow what people say, but often they will still need to watch your face closely when you are talking.

Different types of hearing aid

Hearing aids are made up of the main part of the aid, which goes behind the ear, and an ear mould that fits snugly inside the ear. As your child's ear grows, the audiology department will provide new ear moulds to make sure that they fit well. Special 'mini' models of ear aids are available for babies and small children. There are also models that fit completely in the ear which may be more appealing to older, image conscious children. However, these aids are more prone to breakdown and the whole aid will need to be replaced if the ear grows.

As your child gets older, there are a range of features in modern hearing aids that will help them in different listening situations both at home and at school. One example includes the option of a wireless link with a teacher's microphone or other audio equipment.

The audiologist will explain how to help your child get used to the aids and make the most of their hearing by using features such as volume control. They will also show you how to check the aids and keep them in good working order. Once your child has hearing aids, you will need to visit the audiologist regularly to get the aids checked, the programming adjusted and to ensure they are still working well. They will test your child's hearing with and without the aids so you can see how much they help.

More help

If your child is diagnosed with a hearing problem, your audiologist can refer you to other local services that will offer support and help with everyday life, communication (including sign language or other sign systems), development and education. They can also provide useful equipment for the home and school. Look at the resources available at www.earlysupport. org.uk/modResourcesLibrary/HtmlRenderer/Materials.html. You might also be interested to read *Deafness and Hearing Loss – The Essential Guide* (Need2Know).

Although equipment and hearing aids can help, one of the biggest ways to help your child is to change your behaviour and explain to others how to talk and position themselves to make the most of your child's hearing.

- Make sure your child can see your face when you speak.
- Aim to talk in a quiet place as background noise makes hearing harder.
- Speak clearly, but don't shout.
- Stand still when speaking.
- Repeat your words, if needed.

'Although equipment and hearing aids can help, one of the biggest ways to help your child is to change your behaviour and explain to others how to talk and position themselves to make the most of your child's hearing.'

Sight

Signs of sight problems

If your child is struggling at school or complains of headaches, it is worth getting their eyes examined as children with special needs are more likely to have eye problems. Eye problems can make your child appear clumsy, slow at learning or reluctant to learn. Glasses may solve problems for some children and will make reading, writing and everyday living easier. However, in a few cases an eye examination may show that your child has a problem that needs to be checked by another eye specialist. An eye test can also rule out sight problems as a cause of your child's difficulties.

Getting your child's eyes checked

Every child should get their eyes checked. Even pre-school children can have their eyes examined. Children do not have to be able to talk to get their eyes tested, and the NHS covers the cost of children's sight tests.

If you have never taken your child to see an optometrist, ask around for a recommendation from someone else with children. Some optometrists are particularly interested in helping children with special educational needs. For more information, visit the website of the British Association of Behavioural Optometrists, www.babo.co.uk. To find a practitioner near you, visit Look Up's website, www.lookupinfo.org.

Make the appointment for a time of day when your child is alert, not tired or hungry. Talk to your child about what will happen and practise 'going for an eye test'. You can do this by sitting on a special chair, covering one eye at a time, reading letters or matching shapes and using a torch to show your child how the optometrist might check their eyes.

Who can help?

Optometrist

An optometrist looks for signs of eye disease and assesses your child's eyes to see if they would benefit from glasses.

Orthoptist

An orthoptist specialises in binocular vision, which is the way your child's eyes work together. Orthoptists are usually hospital based and will help if your child has a squint or lazy eye (see page 45).

Ophthalmologist

An ophthalmologist is a doctor who specialises in eye problems. If your GP or optometrist spot something which needs more investigation, you will be referred to hospital to see an ophthalmologist.

The eye examination

It can be daunting entering the room where your child will have their eyes tested. If they have never seen a room like this before, ask if you can have a look round before the actual test. The optometrist will darken the room at points during the test. Discuss this with your child; if it is likely to be a problem, ask the optometrist to adapt what they do.

Your child's history

The optometrist should ask about your child's medical history and medication, and whether anyone in the family has eye problems. Tell the optometrist about any problems your child has with focusing, headaches or other problems.

A routine test

An eye examination contains a number of routine parts. A good optometrist will adapt the tests to your child's needs and abilities.

Checking your child's eye health

The optometrist will shine a bright light close to your child's eyes to check the inside and outside of the eyes for signs of disease.

Checking your child's vision

If your child can read letters, the optometrist will ask them to read a chart. For children who are unsure of their letters, the optometrist can ask them to match the letter they see to a card in their hand. There are also picture charts for children, with images of common objects in varying sizes which can be matched or named. Other charts show simple shapes, so if your child cannot read, ask whether the optometrist has these charts available. The optometrist can also shine a light into your child's eyes to estimate whether they are long- or short-sighted, and 'preferential looking' cards can be used with infants or children who cannot talk.

Checking how your child's eyes work together

The optometrist will ask your child to look at a letter or object and will then cover one eye at a time to see how well their eyes work together.

At the end of the test

Occasionally, the optometrist may ask you to bring your child back for a repeat test after using some eye drops. These drops relax the eye muscles and let the optometrist get a more accurate result. The drops may sting at first and can cause blurred near vision for a few hours.

If your child needs glasses, the optometrist will write you a prescription which will look something like this:

Name and Address of Optometrists

Patient's Name: Jane Smith		Date: 27th June 2008	
Right eye	+2.00/+1.50 x 180	Left eye	+2.25/+1.25 x 175
Signed: An Optician		Recommended retest: 6 months	

Your child may be long-sighted, which is also known as hyperopia. On the spectacle prescription, this would be shown as a plus (+) sign at the start of each line of figures. A long-sighted child has to work harder to focus on close objects. If there is a minus (-) sign at the start of the prescription, your child is short-sighted and will struggle to see distant objects.

The second figure for each eye, after the slash, shows how astigmatic (or rugby ball-shaped) your child's eyes are. Correcting this with glasses can make things clearer at all distances.

Squint and lazy eye

If there is a big difference between your child's eyes, one eye may do more work than the other. Over time, the less-used eye can become lazy, which is known as amblyopia. A squint occurs when the eyes do not work well together and consequently one eye may appear to drift out or in, especially when your child is tired. This can lead to one eye working less well than the other.

If the optometrist thinks your child has a squint or lazy eye, you will be referred to the hospital to see an orthoptist. The orthoptist may suggest 'patching'; covering the better eye to encourage the lazy eye to work. They may prescribe exercises to help your child's eyes work together or your child may need glasses which can help straighten a squint. Some children may also be offered surgery to improve the way the eyes co-ordinate.

Eye disease, low vision and partial sight

A minority of children may have low vision, so even with glasses they will not see as much as other people. If an eye test shows that your child has this sort of problem, you will be referred, via your GP, to an ophthalmologist at the eye hospital. They will check your child's eyes, probably using eye drops to get the best view. They may use a hand held lens to check inside your child's eyes or ask your child to sit still at a slit lamp (a machine that helps the doctor get a good view inside the eye).

Causes of sight problems

'It is important to get your child's eyes and hearing checked regularly. NHS hearing and sight tests are free for children.'

Children who were born prematurely are more likely to have sight problems. Some children may have poor sight due to hereditary or genetic conditions, and others may have suffered damage due to an infection in the womb. Some sight loss can be due to disturbances of the visual pathways from the eye to the back of the brain, and some conditions may not have a known cause.

Glasses and other low visual aids

Children with low vision can use a number of tools to help. At the hospital you should be put in touch with a low vision specialist who can assess your child and recommend magnifiers or other technology to help your child make the most of their vision. The hospital may also be able to point you towards local support groups and a contact at you local social care department, who will assist with equipment to make day-to-day life easier, including speaking clocks and telephones with larger numbers. You should also ask about mobility training to help your child get about independently. This is especially helpful as your child gets older and wants to become more independent. Your LA's education department can help with equipment for school.

For more detailed information, see *Sight Loss – The Essential Guide* (Need2Know).

Summing Up

It is important to get your child's eyes and hearing checked regularly. NHS hearing and sight tests are free for children. Spectacles or a hearing aid can often help children who have special educational needs and can make it easier for them to learn.

Here are some ideas for actions to help you and your child:

☐ Has your child had their hearing checked? If they haven't, and you suspect there is a problem, talk to your GP.

☐ Has your child had their eyes examined? If not, book an appointment with an optometrist.

☐ If your child has a hearing or sight problem, are you in touch with your local social care department? They may be able to help with equipment to make day-to-day life easier.

☐ Talk to your LA's education department about help at school and specialist teachers for children with hearing or vision problems.

Chapter Five

Physical Disabilities

More than 7% of children with a Statement of Special Educational Needs have a physical disability. Conditions like cerebral palsy or spina bifida affect children in a range of ways and can cause:

- Problems with mobility.
- Difficulty concentrating.
- Co-ordination problems.

Who can help?

Physiotherapist (physio): a physiotherapist helps children and young people with movement disorders, disability or illness to reach their full potential through physical intervention, advice and support. They can help your child to become more independent and develop their physical fitness. Anything the physio does will work best if it is done in co-operation with you, your child's school and other professionals that help look after your child.

Depending on your child's needs and the local services available, you may see a physio at a hospital or clinic. Some may visit schools or your home. If you think your child needs to see a physio, ask your GP for a referral or speak to your child's specialist doctor.

What the physiotherapist does

Assessment

The physiotherapist should ask you all about your child's life. It will help if they get information from your child's school and other health professionals who may have worked with your child. By looking at your child, they will check their:

- Balance.
- Co-ordination.
- Motor development.
- Posture.
- Quality of movement.
- Strength.

When your child has been assessed, the physiotherapist will tell you if they think your child will benefit from physiotherapy and how it might help. You should also get a written report.

Helping your child

The physiotherapist can help your child in a number of ways. They may:

- Give your child therapy alone or in a group.
- Recommend special swimming.
- Train others, like you or your child's classroom assistant, to help your child with their physical development.
- Advise on and supply special equipment.

Who can help?

Occupational therapist (OT): this therapist will work with you to see if your child has difficulties with social and practical skills. The occupational therapist can work out ways to help your child maximise their potential in everyday life. They will work with you and your child, the school and any social care or health professionals who work with your child too. They may come to your child's home, school or nursery, or you may visit a clinic.

What an occupational therapist does

Assessment

The occupational therapist will ask you about your child's health, development and daily activities. They may get more information from your school or nursery too. By watching your child and asking questions, they will discover how your child:

- Balances.
- Does fine motor tasks.
- Eats.
- Gets dressed.
- Gets on with others.
- Goes to the toilet.
- Holds a pencil or scissors.
- Moves.
- Plays.
- Senses touch.

Helping your child

After the assessment you should get a written report, which will also go to your GP. The occupational therapist will let you know if and how your child might benefit from occupational therapy. The occupational therapist may help by:

- Offering your child therapy, either one-to-one or in a group.
- Training you and other care workers.
- Recommending special equipment to help your child do day-to-day tasks and learn.

With both physiotherapy and occupational therapy, any help will be given for a period of time and then your child's progress will be assessed. The therapist will explain to you if your child needs more therapy, would benefit from a break or has achieved their potential at the time.

Physiotherapists and occupational therapists need to be registered with the Health Professions Council. You can check the registration of a physiotherapist at www.hpc-uk.org. See also the Chartered Society of Physiotherapy site at www.csp.org.uk. For the physiotherapists' code of practice and more information on occupational therapists, visit the College of Occupational Therapists' site at www.cot.org.uk. There is also a National Association of Paediatric Occupational Therapists, visit www.napot.co.uk for further details.

Making life easier

The right equipment can make life enormously easier. Talk to your GP if you are unsure of where to start. You can get help with equipment from the NHS, your local social care department and your LA's education department.

For mobility equipment, such as a wheelchair, scooter or bike, go to the NHS wheelchair service. Your local occupational therapist or physiotherapist can point you in the right direction and help you find the service you need. If you know your child will benefit from a mobility aid but the NHS won't provide it, you can contact the charity Whizz-Kidz (see help list for contact details.)

'The right equipment can make life enormously easier. Talk to your GP if you are unsure where to start. You can get help with equipment from the NHS, your local social care department and your LA's education department.'

Better access at school

Your child's school must make reasonable adaptations so your child gets access to all parts of school life. They may need to make plans to change the physical environment, the way your child gets information or the way they deliver the curriculum. It could be something as simple as:

- Making sure your child's lessons are all on the ground floor.
- Changing paint colours on steps or improving lighting for children with limited vision.
- Adding carpet to keep background noise down if you child has impaired hearing.
- Making timetables or handouts available in large print, on tape, in Braille, etc.
- Reorganising the classroom seating plan.

Technology

The right technology can help your child learn. Ask your child's school about:

- Touch-screen computers, joysticks and trackerballs.
- Easy-to-use keyboards.
- Interactive whiteboards.
- Text-to-speech software.
- Braille-translation software.
- Software that connects words with pictures or symbols.

If your child has a statement, it should tell you and the school what technology should be provided to help your child make the most of their learning time.

'Your child's school must make reasonable adaptations so your child gets access to all parts of school life.'

Getting about

If you need help with travel, you may want to find out about the Motability car scheme. If your child gets Higher Rate Mobility Allowance, you can use this to get a new car through the lease scheme. The car insurance and servicing is covered by the scheme too. If you don't get this allowance, according to the government website www.direct.gov.uk, you may be entitled if your child is:

- Aged three or more and unable or virtually unable to walk.

- Aged three or more and assessed to be both 100% disabled because of loss of eyesight and not less than 80% disabled because of deafness.

- Aged three or more and severely mentally impaired with severe behavioural problems and qualifies for the highest rate of care component.

- Aged five and in need of guidance or supervision when walking out of doors.

Your LA may help get your child to school. Their decision will depend on how old your child is and their level of disability. You might also be able to get help with your costs for taking your child to school or an escort for your child. Ask your LA for more information.

Summing Up

Some children with special educational needs may also have physical disabilities. There is help available to make your life and your child's easier. Therapists can help your child develop to their full potential and help you access the right equipment for your child. You may also be able to get help with transport.

Here is a quick checklist so you can plan what action to try next:

☐ Has your child been for physiotherapy? Ask your GP or specialist if it might help.

☐ What about occupational therapy? Check if this will help your child.

☐ Ask the therapists for advice about supporting your child's development.

☐ Are you getting the benefits your child is entitled to? Check out www.direct.gov.uk or visit your local Jobcentre Plus.

☐ Do you need help with transport? Find out about Motability and speak to your LA about help getting to school.

Chapter Six

Hereditary and Genetic Conditions

If your child has a genetic or hereditary condition, they may have a range of additional needs. In this chapter we look at some of the more common conditions and the sort of help that might be relevant for you and your child.

Finding out about your child's condition

Some parents-to-be will find out that their child has a risk of a genetic disorder during pregnancy screening, but screening only gives you an indication that there may be a chance of a condition occurring. You may have realised that your child was different immediately after the birth, medical staff may have raised a concern or it may become apparent as your child grows older and develops differently or at a different rate to their peers.

This chapter only touches on a few of the most common conditions and gives suggestions for where to go for more help and to get in touch with others affected by each disorder:

- Duchenne muscular dystrophy and other musculoskeletal disorders.

- Down's syndrome and other chromosomal conditions.

- Fragile X syndrome.

Duchenne muscular dystrophy and other musculoskeletal disorders

Factfile

- There are more than 20 types of muscular dystrophy, all of which are caused by faults in genes.

- Duchenne muscular dystrophy affects boys, but females can be carriers.

- In almost half of cases, the gene defect occurs without anyone in the family being a carrier.

- The condition causes a gradual increase in muscle weakness. Affected boys show difficulty in walking while toddlers may struggle to climb stairs, run or jump. Those affected may also have learning difficulties or behavioural difficulties.

- The condition worsens and by eight to 11 years of age, boys may be unable to walk and will have a shortened life expectancy.

- There are ways to help manage the condition but no way yet to stop the loss of muscle cells.

A child with muscular dystrophy may not need any help in the early stages, and a physiotherapist can help as the condition progresses. However, you will need to see a specialist on a regular basis to watch for any problems with the heart and breathing muscles so they can be treated to reduce long-term problems. The Joseph Patrick Trust provides grants towards equipment and wheelchairs – see chapter 5 if you are at the stage where you need help with your child's mobility.

You should look at local primary schools as most children with muscular dystrophy cope well with mainstream school at this stage. As your son gets older, you may want to help him develop skills, hobbies and interests that he can continue to enjoy, despite lack of muscle strength. A computer can also be an essential tool.

If your son wants to progress to further or higher education, he may also be able to get a grant towards equipment, assistance, travel or accommodation from the Snowdon Award Scheme. The Muscular Dystrophy Campaign also has information on support groups and other neuromuscular conditions, so it's well worth investigating. See chapter 11 for more about getting help at school.

Down's syndrome and other chromosomal conditions

Down's syndrome is one of the most common genetic conditions, caused by the presence of an extra chromosome in pair 21. It is not yet known what causes this extra chromosome to occur, but it happens more often if a mother is older, with the risk rising to 1 in 20 in women over 45.

Children with this syndrome usually have distinctive features, which means that once your baby has been delivered, you or the medical staff may suspect that the condition is present.

As they grow, you may find that your child has some developmental delay and is slow to sit, stand or walk, due to poor muscle tone. Your child may also take longer to learn to talk and it is important to check your child's sight and hearing as they may have an increased risk of problems. See chapter 2 for more on developmental delay and chapter 4 for more on sight and hearing.

Most children with Down's syndrome attend a mainstream school at the primary stage, where they thrive from accessing their education alongside their peers. Sometimes children move to more specialist provision at secondary level, although with the promotion of inclusive education, this is changing. Find out how your local schools would provide the extra support that your child might need and get in touch with the Down's Syndrome Association for more help. See chapter 11 for more on choosing a school and getting additional help.

Edwards' syndrome is caused by three chromosomes instead of two in pair 18. It is also called trisomy 18 and is the next most common chromosomal abnormality after Down's syndrome. Around 80% of those affected are female and around half of embryos with the syndrome will die before the pregnancy is completed. About half of those babies who are born alive will die in their first year. In a small number of cases not all genes have the extra chromosome, which means that there are fewer abnormalities.

Children with Edwards' syndrome can have developmental delays and physical impairments, such as breathing and feeding difficulties. Contact S.O.F.T UK (Support Organisation for Trisomy 13/18 and Related Disorders) for help from other parents who have experience of a child with the condition. Contact a Family also has information on the syndrome. See help list for contact details.

Fragile X

Fragile X is another genetic condition, which occurs in around 1 in 4,000 boys and 1 in 8,000 girls. It can be more severe in boys and causes a varying degree of learning difficulty. Children may have problems in processing new information, short-term memory, dealing with numbers and organisation and planning. Your child can also have speech and language difficulties (see chapter 1), challenging behaviour (see chapter 9) and co-ordination problems. They may struggle with social situations and display other characteristics that are similar to autism, but they can be affectionate.

Fragile X can be carried by mothers and fathers. A woman has a 50-50 chance of passing the chromosome on, with a one in three chance of a female baby being affected and an almost certain chance of a male baby having the condition. Men can pass the chromosome on to a female baby, but not to a male one.

Find out more from the Fragile X Society, which offers support, information and friendship to families whose children and relatives have the syndrome.

Getting advice and counselling

You may wish to speak to your GP about accessing some form of counselling for your family. It can be difficult to acknowledge that your child's condition is a genetic one and many parents report feelings of guilt. It is vital that you speak to each other honestly about your feelings around diagnosis and don't blame each other.

'You may wish to speak to your GP about accessing some form of counselling for your family. It can be difficult to acknowledge that your child's condition is a genetic one and many parents report feelings of guilt. It is vital that you speak to each other honestly about your feelings around diagnosis and don't blame each other.'

You could also use a befriending scheme to talk to parents who have been in the same situation. The details for Scope's Face 2 Face befriending scheme and all the organisations mentioned can be found in the useful contacts section at the end of this book.

Talking to your child about their condition

As your child gets older, they may ask you more about their condition. Siblings may also ask about what is happening. Listen to what your child is saying and try to answer what they are asking. Your child may have picked up more than you think during medical appointments and may need to share this with you. Let them know that you are always willing to talk and perhaps set aside a little time each day or week to listen to them.

More help

It can be hard to find a balance between looking after your child and giving attention to their siblings, but sharing experiences can help you when you are struggling. Get in touch with an organisation like Contact a Family who can help you link up with others in similar situations. Home-Start can put you in touch with someone to help you by listening and talking, helping with the children, giving you a break and helping you use local services and resources. See chapter 8 for more on family life.

'It can be hard to find a balance between looking after your child and giving attention to their siblings, but sharing experiences can help you when you are struggling.'

Summing Up

It can be devastating to hear that your child has a genetic condition and you may feel guilty that they have inherited it from you or angry at your partner. Get some help from a counsellor and link up with a support group.

Here are some ideas for what to do next:

- [ ] Make time for yourself, your partner and your other children.
- [ ] Think about asking for counselling.
- [ ] Ask for help from an organisation like Home-Start or Contact a Family.
- [ ] Remember to celebrate the things your child can do.

For more specific information on Down's syndrome, see *Down's Syndrome – The Essential Guide*.

Chapter Seven

Specific Learning Difficulties

Does your child seem to do well in some areas, but struggle in others? If you are perplexed by your child's issues with reading or writing, have you looked into whether they have a specific learning difficulty (SpLD)? Children who have been labelled disruptive or slow may simply be struggling with a condition such as dyslexia. Those who are called clumsy or disorganised may have dyspraxia.

Getting your child assessed and finding the reason behind their difficulties can help you and your child's teacher work out the best way to help them learn and enjoy school too. Children with SpLDs can be aware that they are different and some may find it hard to make friends. Early identification of a problem can stop your child feeling that people are labelling them stupid and will avoid damage to their self-esteem.

What are specific learning difficulties?

Specific learning difficulties (SpLDs) cover a group of conditions. Most people will have heard of dyslexia, but if your child struggles more with writing or maths, you may want to investigate dysgraphia or dyscalculia. Your child may have just one condition or could be experiencing problems due to a combination. See also chapters 2 and 3, as SpLDs can co-exist with global developmental delay and autistic spectrum disorders.

'Children with SpLDs can be aware that they are different and some may find it hard to make friends. Early identification of a problem can stop your child feeling that people are labelling them stupid and will avoid damage to their self-esteem.'

Dyspraxia

At least one child in every class will have dyspraxia, according to the Dyspraxia Foundation. This developmental co-ordination disorder can mean that your child has problems with:

Tick if your child shows these signs:

- ☐ Hand-eye co-ordination.
- ☐ Fine motor movement such as pen control or handling small objects.
- ☐ Putting things in order.

They may struggle with their sense of time or direction and have a poor memory for lists, events or names. Dyspraxia is more likely to occur in boys.

Dyslexia

Due to the way their brain processes language, children with dyslexia can have problems with reading, writing and even spoken language. Children can also struggle with order and organisation, finding it harder than their peers to remember lists and tasks. Around 4% of the population may have dyslexia.

Dysgraphia

If your child is generally bright but cannot get thoughts down on paper, they may have dysgraphia. This condition can mean that a child who communicates ideas well when talking will struggle when asked to put them in writing.

Dyscalculia

Dyscalculia occurs when a child struggles to get to grips with numbers. They may not have difficulties with all mathematics, but perhaps reverse numbers or have a mental block when it comes to learning sequences, times tables or formulae.

Signs that there may be a problem

Children vary and will have both good and bad days. If your child does well in some areas but has constant struggles in others, look out for some of the following signs. Think about whether other members of the family have shown these sorts of problems too.

Signs of dyspraxia

Tick if your child shows these signs:

- [ ] Delay in learning to stand, walk or speak.
- [ ] Difficulties with ball games, running or riding a bike.
- [ ] Fidgeting, leg swinging, inability to sit still.
- [ ] Knocking things over, falling, spilling, bumping into things.
- [ ] Problems with stairs.
- [ ] Problems dressing, difficulties with buttons and laces.
- [ ] Difficulties with puzzles and construction games.
- [ ] Lack of interest in or immature attempts at arts and crafts.
- [ ] Lack of organisational skills, poor memory and difficulties following instructions.
- [ ] Lack of awareness of danger.
- [ ] Easily distracted.
- [ ] Finds it hard to make friends.

Signs of dyslexia

Tick if your child shows these signs:

- [ ] Mixing up letters like d and b, u and n or m and n.

- [ ] Confusing letters which sound the same like v, f and th.
- [ ] Reversing or transposing words like was-saw or left-felt.
- [ ] Often confuses directional words (up and down, in and out).
- [ ] Problems with sequences and patterns.
- [ ] Difficulties remembering days of the week, the alphabet or rhymes.

Signs of dysgraphia

Tick if your child shows these signs:

- [ ] Illegible writing.
- [ ] Poor spelling.
- [ ] Lack of stamina for writing.
- [ ] Unfinished or variable letter forms and sizes.
- [ ] Mixes upper and lower case letters.

Signs of dyscalculia

Tick if your child shows these signs:

- [ ] Difficulties with mathematical calculations.
- [ ] Reversing numbers.
- [ ] Problems with laying out answers in a particular format.
- [ ] Difficulties with times tables or formulae.
- [ ] Problems reading and understanding maths questions.
- [ ] Struggles with directions like left and right.
- [ ] Difficulties learning about money.
- [ ] Problems keeping track of time, past and future.

For more detailed lists of signs, see *Dyslexia and other Learning Difficulties – A Parent's Guide* (Need2Know).

Getting your child assessed

Your child can be tested from around four years of age for dyslexia and doesn't need to be able to read or write. Private tests cost from around £30 to £500, varying from a quick 20 minute assessment to a full assessment by an educational psychologist who can also measure your child's IQ.

Less is known about dysgraphia and dyscalculia, but for all three conditions you can also ask for an assessment through your child's school; LA's employ educational psychologists to do this so you won't have to pay, but there may be a long waiting list. You will also need the school's agreement that your child needs assessing. Online assessments are useful to help identify that your child may have a condition like dyslexia, but they can't replace professional input.

An assessment should give you an idea of your child's strengths and weaknesses, checking their levels of comprehension, writing, spelling and reading. You will find out whether your child can perform better or whether they are performing at the level that is right for them. If tested by an educational psychologist, you should get recommendations on how to help your child learn. The British Dyslexia Association has a list of assessment tests and contact details. (See help list.)

If you have concerns that your child has dyspraxia, speak to your GP or health visitor for under fives, or the school nurse, school doctor or special needs co-ordinator for school age children. You may be referred to a paediatrician or a Child Development Centre. You may also want to ask if your child will benefit from assessment and therapy from a psychologist, physiotherapist, an SLT or occupational therapist.

Who can help?

Educational psychologist: educational psychologists can work privately or for your LA. They specialise in dealing with learning difficulties and social or emotional problems encountered by children and young people who are in school or college.

More help

Dyslexia and other SpLD's can't be cured, but most children will benefit from a multi-sensory approach to learning. By using their sense of touch, hearing and sight, saying words and feeling their sound, the child is better able to learn. This applies whether your child has problems with reading, writing or numbers, and explains why using a tactile tool like a sand tray for writing numbers or letters can work well for some children. Learning using phonics, teaching children to connect sounds with letters or groups of letters, can help children with reading. As children get older, look at alternatives to the hard slog of reading and writing, like using a computer or listening to an audiobook. They won't be able to avoid all reading and writing, but finding alternatives can help them keep up.

Read on for more help with SpLDs. Don't forget to get your child's sight and hearing checked too (see chapter 4 for more information).

Help for dyspraxia

'If your child has dyspraxia, help them develop confidence and encourage them as much as possible. Break down tasks that they struggle with into small steps and make sure that they have time to finish one thing before moving on to the next.

At school, sports lessons can be a problem area: the child can feel that they are always last. Ask the teacher to think of activities that will help your child build their skills and to offer non-competitive alternatives to team games, like yoga or aerobics. Physiotherapy and occupational therapy can help motor and co-ordination skills. At home, practise games to help your child's co-ordination. Think about balance, e.g. standing on one leg, and move onto jumping and hopping games too.

Help for dyslexia

There are various systems which claim to help children with dyslexia. You may want to look at 'over learning' – the repetitive study of something until it becomes second nature. Computer programs which give instant feedback and

'If your child has dyspraxia, help them develop confidence and encourage them as much as possible. Break down tasks that they struggle with into small steps and make sure that they have time to finish one thing before moving onto the next.'

provide reinforcement can get children interested in learning and boost what they remember in the long term. See *Dyslexia and other Learning Difficulties – A Parent's Guide* by Maria Chivers for plenty of recommendations for specific programs and software.

Help for dysgraphia

There are different approaches to helping a child with dysgraphia. Some children can benefit from practising. Look for handwriting practice books, check the way your child holds their pen and see if a pencil grip can help. You can also help your child develop better control of their movements by forming letters in a sand tray, tracing or threading. Maria Chivers suggests juggling and swimming can also help.

As well as helping your child develop their writing skills as far as possible, you may also want to look into using a computer. Teaching a child with dysgraphia to touch type can take a lot of pressure off, especially as they get older and need to hand in homework for assessment. A child who can type is able to concentrate on their answers and ideas without being limited by their writing skills.

Talk to your child's teacher and SENCO about achieving a balance between helping them improve their writing and letting them learn more freely by using a computer. Watch out for any different alternative therapies for dyslexia and ask for independent research to show how the therapy works before investing in it for your child.

Help for dyscalculia

If your child has dyscalculia, talk to their teacher and SENCO about different ways to help them understand the concepts they struggle with. Find out what they are learning at school and ask if there are essentials you can repeat and practise at home. The teacher may have ideas for different approaches to use in class or you can ask them to take time to check that your child is clear and recap if necessary. Your child may benefit from one-to-one help when learning how to memorise mathematical facts and other study skills. Talk to them about breaking tasks down into parts, then working through step-by-step to complete them.

Children with dyscalculia can find a multi-sensory approach helpful. They may understand more if they do sums in a sand tray or form numbers using play dough. Think about ways to build your child's confidence with mathematical ideas, like measuring ingredients to bake a cake, guessing how many toy cars are in their garage or handling money when you are shopping. The British Dyslexia Association has a page with resources to help children with dyscalculia (see help list for further information).

Making life easier

If your child is struggling at school, talk to the class teacher or SENCO. See chapter 11 to find out about Individual Education Plans (IEPs) or getting a Statement of Special Educational Needs. You may want to look for a specialist teacher with an SLD qualification who can give your child some private tutoring, or you could consider switching schools altogether.

Identify particular areas where your child struggles at home and work out ways to make it easier. If dressing takes ages, put clothes out in order and avoid tricky fastenings. Keep to a routine as much as possible.

Help your child feel good about what they do well. Help them develop their own hobbies and interests in areas where they are not compared to siblings or schoolmates. This can help your child value what they can do rather than focusing on areas where they can't keep up.

'Identify particular areas where your child struggles at home and work out ways to make it easier. If dressing takes ages, put clothes out in order and avoid tricky fastenings. Keep to a routine as much as possible.'

Summing Up

Specific learning difficulties (SpLDs) are relatively common and may be found in combination. There are strategies to help your child improve their skills and learn ways to study more easily. Get help as soon as possible before your child starts feeling bad about always struggling to keep up.

Here is a quick checklist of actions to try next:

☐ If you are worried about your child's reading, writing, physical co-ordination or grasp of numbers, look at the list of signs in this chapter and note down a list of the ones that apply to your child.

☐ Talk to your GP, health visitor or the school SENCO to start the process of getting your child assessed.

☐ At the assessment ask for ways you can help your child learn at home and what the teacher can do in class.

☐ Visit the website for the British Dyslexia Association or the Dyspraxia Foundation for lots of tips. Look for local groups to join too.

☐ Help your child develop different hobbies and interests.

Chapter Eight

Family Life

Having a child with a special educational need can have a significant effect on family life. This chapter looks at how to develop better ways to cope as a family, recognising the stresses that your family may face and the importance of celebrating the good things about your situation.

When your child has an additional need, it can impact on the whole family. One parent may no longer be able to work, having to take the role of carer; there may be numerous hospital appointments to attend; housing may need to be adapted to cater for physical disabilities; and it may feel like you have entered a whole new world. As a result, it is essential that you develop support networks for yourself and for your family.

Parents

Parenting is a difficult task and can seem even more challenging when your child has a special need. If you are in a relationship, it can be hard to keep it alive when there are so many demands upon your time.

Lorna's relationship broke down when her son was three years old: 'Charlie was always in and out of hospital; I had to do all the caring while Mick went out to work. By the time he got home, I couldn't face going through what the consultant had said or showing him how to give the medication. I just got on and did it and then felt angry that it was all down to me, which led to rows.'

Follow these simple tips in order to look after your relationship:

- Set aside time each evening to talk about your day to make sure that problems don't build up.

- Recognise that men and women communicate for different purposes. Men generally communicate to solve problems, women to share feelings. Women need to explain that they want their feelings to be heard, while men need to understand that they are not being asked to solve the problems but to listen to the feelings.

- If your partner misses a hospital appointment, ask the consultant if you could record it using a dictaphone. That way you don't have to explain the consultation and the parent who wasn't there can hear everything.

- If your partner can't make appointments, ask them to make a list of the things they want you to raise.

- Celebrate the positives and the small steps of progress that your child makes.

- Remember that you are lovers, not just parents. Can you organise a night out? If not, have a regular evening in where you have time as a couple, eating a nice meal or watching a DVD.

Non-resident parents

If you and your child's other parent live apart, it can make communicating more difficult. Ideas to make life easier include:

- Ask for papers from school and medical appointments to be sent to both houses.

- Keep a diary that can be passed between the two houses, showing appointments and sharing information. This cuts down on the need to keep phoning and helps if your relationship is strained. A diary can ensure your child gets looked after consistently too.

Need2Know

Grandparents

Grandparents can be a source of support or, at times, a source of stress. They may find it difficult to come to terms with a diagnosis. They are not only worrying about their grandchild but about their own child.

> Jane states: 'I get back from school after a difficult meeting and have to relay all the information to Jake's dad. No sooner have I done that and my mother phones and I have to go through it all over again. Then she gets upset and I end up counselling her while I'm left feeling numb, exhausted and unsupported.'

What can you do?

- Explain to grandparents that sometimes you don't feel emotionally ready to share details of meetings immediately. You will share them as soon as you can.

- Offer them information about your child's special educational need that they can take away and read.

- Be honest with them; tell them when you are finding it difficult to cope and ask for practical help.

- If possible, put them in touch with other grandparents locally who have a grandchild with a special need.

Siblings

Having a brother or sister with a special educational need can be a positive experience. Elaine's brother has Down's syndrome. She says: 'I took a real interest in Tom's welfare and found out all I could about Down's syndrome. It made me have a much more mature outlook compared to my peers and I wanted to be involved in the decisions that affected his life.'

'Grandparents can be a source of support or, at times, a source of stress.'

Being a sibling of a child with a special educational need can also be challenging. Siblings report facing a range of difficulties due to their brother or sister's additional needs, including:

- Inability to complete homework due to lack of personal space.

- Always being second to their sibling in having their needs met.

- Feelings of anxiety regarding their sibling/family's situation.

- Sleep deprivation (see chapter 10).

- Inability to bring friends home due to feeling embarrassed about their sibling's needs.

- Fear of bullying.

- Worry about the future – who will take care of their brother or sister in the long term?

Families with a child with special educational needs may suffer financial problems, which can affect siblings too. See chapter 12 for more on financial help.

Supporting your other children

Here are some tips to support your other children:

- Tell their school about their sibling's special educational need, particularly if it may have an impact on homework, sleep, access to social activities, etc.

- Encourage the sibling to discuss their anxieties. You are in a position to empathise with their situation.

- Ask the sibling how much information they want about the special educational need. Some siblings don't want to find out more, while others are keen to read every piece of information.

- Discuss the future. Make it clear that you do not expect the sibling to take on parental responsibility for your other child.

- Find out about local sibling support groups. The charity Sibs www.sibs.org.uk is for brothers and sisters of disabled children and adults.

Friends

Friends may find it difficult to know how to react to the news that your child has a special educational need. Some parents report that friends avoid them as they don't know what to say or don't talk about their own children's achievements. Friends are a vital support network for your family, so make sure that they understand how much you value their friendship.

- Explain to them that you don't want the friendship to change.
- Ask them to be honest with you and ask questions if they feel they would like to know more about your child's needs or how to handle situations with your child.
- Tell them that you want to hear about their children too.

Who can help?

Respite

All parents need time off. Ask your social worker about respite opportunities. If you feel uneasy about placing your child into a respite home, ask whether there is a family respite scheme where the child stays with another family. If your local social care department cannot offer respite, ask your family and friends if they can look after your child for a couple of hours so that you get time on your own.

Voluntary groups

Local groups can be a tremendous source of support. There is a whole range of services on offer: from putting you in contact with other parents, to practical advice around benefits. Details of such groups will be available at your local library.

'When parenting a child with special needs, it is vital to remain positive. Take some time out to think about the positive impact that your child has had on your lives and to celebrate their achievements.'

Support groups

There is a range of support groups:

- Local groups meet on a regular basis in your area. Groups vary, so it is worth telephoning to ask about their format. Is it a campaigning group? Do members meet and socialise with the children?

- National groups may focus on the special need that your child has and can be a source of telephone help and occasional meetings.

- Online groups, forums and chat rooms allow parents around the globe to offer each other support and information. A great way of getting in touch with other parents if you can't get out much, online groups allow you to find people who have children with similar additional needs, even if your child's condition is rare.

- Befriending services train parents to befriend other parents in order to offer emotional support.

Counsellors

If life is becoming increasingly difficult, discuss counselling with your partner. Your GP should be able to refer you, although there is often a waiting list. You can also look for a counsellor privately – your GP may have some contacts or you can look in your local telephone directory. Remember to ask a counsellor whether they have experience in helping parents of children with special needs.

The positives

When parenting a child with special needs, it is vital to remain positive. Take some time out to think about the positive impact that your child has had on your lives and to celebrate their achievements. Make a book or display board of good memories, and note down the great things your child does. Write down when someone says something positive about your child or when you see them do something new. Glue in photos and drawings too. You can look through this when you are feeling down or share it with your child to help you both see all the good things they do.

Summing Up

Be honest when dealing with family and friends; state clearly to them how you are feeling and how you wish to be treated. Recognise that siblings may be anxious too and make sure that the whole family has adequate support systems in place.

Have a look at this list for ideas on what to do next:

- ☐ Make time for your relationship. Try to listen to each other every day.
- ☐ Talk to your child's siblings and listen to how they feel.
- ☐ Find out about respite care. Even if you feel you are coping now, it can be useful to know what support is there when you need it.
- ☐ Ask your library about support groups. Look locally or online.
- ☐ Make a 'special memories' book or display to celebrate family life.

Chapter Nine

Behaviour Difficulties at Home

All children exhibit challenging behaviour at some point during their lives. For children with special needs, it may be difficult to decide what is and what isn't acceptable behaviour. It is important to use strategies that your child can understand and respond to positively. Dealing with behaviour difficulties can be stressful, but having a plan of action can significantly reduce that stress and leave you feeling more in control.

This chapter looks at the different behaviour difficulties that you may encounter. It will help you identify triggers for the behaviour and to use simple strategies to effectively deal with it. It is important that strategies are used consistently by everybody involved with the child. Children respond well to boundaries once they are firmly in place, but it is not unusual for a child's behaviour to worsen when you begin to modify it; they are simply pushing to see how far your boundaries will shift. When they realise that they are firmly set, improvements will begin to take place.

Different behaviours

There are a wide range of behaviours that children can exhibit including spitting, being aggressive towards others and self harming. Write a list of the sort of behaviour that your child shows which causes you concern.

> Types of behaviour..
> ....
> ....
> ....
> ....
> ....

Consider your child's behaviour when you are out and about. Will they walk appropriately near roads? Is their behaviour worse when in busy places such as supermarkets? What exactly do they do?

If your child is at school or nursery, ask if your child demonstrates any challenging behaviour while they are there. Find out how the school/nursery deals with this so that you can use some of their ideas in the home.

Changing behaviours

You will now be clear about the kind of behaviour that you are looking to change. Your child may demonstrate more than one type of challenging behaviour, but it is important that you only deal with modifying one behaviour at a time. Decide as a family which behaviour you think will be the easiest to deal with and choose that as your first priority.

> Our priority...

The ABC chart

Children misbehave for a reason – it is their way of telling you that there is a problem. Sometimes it is difficult to work out why children are behaving in certain ways and it is helpful to identify a trigger for the behaviour.

Need2Know

An ABC chart is a simple way of recording how your child behaves and then using the information to work out why it happens. It can help you spot a pattern in the behaviour. For example, it may occur at a certain time of day when your child is tired or hungry.

'A' stands for antecedent. This means that you need to look at what happened immediately prior to the bad behaviour beginning. 'B' is for behaviour and requires you to describe exactly what the behaviour was and how you responded to it. 'C' is for consequence, which means you need to explain what your child got out of the behaviour.

This following case study gives an example of how to use the chart.

Lewis and Oliver are brothers. They are playing with cars on the floor. This has been going on for 10 minutes, Lewis is three years old and Oliver is five years old. Lewis sees Oliver's car and takes it from him, Oliver snatches it back. Lewis then screams and bites his own arm repeatedly. At this point their mother intervenes, picking Lewis up and cuddling him while examining his arm.

Antecedent What happened immediately prior to the behaviour?	The boys were playing on the floor for 10 minutes with cars. Lewis may be bored with the activity and it is time for his afternoon nap.
Behaviour What behaviour was seen? How did you respond?	Lewis takes a car from Oliver. Oliver snatches the car back. Lewis screams and bites himself. Mother picks Lewis up, giving him attention for his behaviour.
Consequence What did the child gain from the behaviour?	Lewis got attention from his mother and a change of activity.

The ABC Chart   Date: 9th August   Time: 2.35pm

Taking the information that we have collected, we can see that Lewis was in fact rewarded for his behaviour. Lewis will therefore learn that biting his arm gets him the attention that he wants. Next time he wants adult attention he may well resort to biting himself.

Now fill in the ABC chart for the behaviour you want to work on with your child. You may want to copy the table so you can use it a number of times.

In our example it is easy to see the pattern. You may need to fill in several ABC charts for your child before you spot a pattern. Can you identify a trigger for the behaviour? If you can, you will be able to identify when the behaviour might occur and can start thinking of ways to avoid the trigger situation.

Antecedent What happened immediately prior to the behaviour?	
Behaviour What behaviour was seen? How did you respond?	
Consequence What did the child gain from the behaviour?	

The ABC Chart   **Date:**   **Time:**

Need2Know

Now that you have identified the behaviours that are causing concern, it is time to develop strategies to ensure that they are reduced.

Specific praise

Praise your child and explain to them exactly which part of their behaviour you are pleased with. 'Good girl' is too general for them to understand. Instead, say something along the lines of 'I like the way that you are sharing your toys, that is really good'. Try to comment positively on your child showing the behaviour that you are trying to encourage.

Catch them being good

When behaviour is at its most challenging, it can be hard to find something positive to say. Make a real effort to notice them being good – even if they are quietly looking at a book for just a few minutes, tell them that you love the way that they are sitting calmly.

Use a reward system

Reward charts are a simple way of letting children know that you are pleased with their behaviour. Before using this system, make sure they understand that a star on their chart is a reward and never take stars down from a chart. This is a positive reward system, so using sad faces or removing stars devalues it and can result in children no longer feeling good about their chart.

Ideas for rewards:

- Buy some stickers. If your child enjoys wearing stickers, you could buy a pack to reward good behaviour.
- Reward coins are tokens that your child can collect. They are ideal for using when out and about.

Rewards should be given immediately so that children understand exactly what they are being rewarded for. Make it clear when you give the reward, for example: 'This sticker is for eating your dinner so nicely'.

Ignore bad behaviour

It is incredibly hard to do at times, but if you give your child attention then they have received a reward for their efforts. If your child is not in danger of hurting themselves, others or damaging property, withdraw your eye contact from them. They need to learn that they will get your attention when they are behaving appropriately.

Give verbal reminders to your child

If they are beginning to become unruly, a clear 'No, we do not throw toys' may be enough to remind them to stop. If your child has limited understanding, you could use photographs, signs or symbols to support what you are saying.

'It is incredibly hard to do at times, but if you give your child attention then they have received a reward for their efforts.'

Using your child's name

Make sure your child has your attention by starting each sentence with their name. Make your instructions to them short and to the point. For example, 'Please do not kick your brother, you might hurt him' should be changed to 'Daniel, no kicking'.

Label the act, never the child

For example, saying 'Ben you are a naughty boy for hitting Sam' labels Ben when actually it is the behaviour that should be labelled. So this should be changed to 'Ben, hitting Sam was naughty'. Labelling children negatively can seriously damage their self-esteem.

Whatever approach you use, be consistent. Once you have picked one of the ideas, try to use it each time, otherwise you are sending out confused signals to your child.

Time out

Sometimes it may be necessary to remove your child from a situation in order to calm down. Many parents use the 'naughty step', but there are far more positive places to send your child. How about using a 'thinking chair'? This is a chair where they can sit for a designated amount of time and think about their behaviour and the consequences it has had. Or you could create a 'peaceful place' where they can sit and calm down in a tranquil environment. You may just need a cushion and a favourite blanket in a quiet corner for this.

Tips for using time out:

- State that it is time to sit out in a calm manner.
- Only use it to deal with the most challenging behaviour.
- Use it for the minimum amount of time possible.
- Invest in a sand timer to give your child a visual idea for how long they should be sitting there. Watching the sand flow also helps many children to calm down more quickly.
- This should not be a humiliating experience or a punishment; this should be a genuine opportunity for your child to calm down.
- Once your child has returned, the incident should be forgotten.

Sanctions

Sanctions should be used as a last resort in behaviour management. If you use sanctions too often, they will fail to work. It is a good idea to consider what sanctions you may use prior to the incident. Sanctions that you could consider would be:

- Not allowing a favourite TV programme.
- Stopping the child from engaging in a favourite activity. For example, using the computer.
- Not going on a planned outing.
- Confiscating a favourite toy.

Remember that rewards are far more effective than sanctions.

Behaviour outside the home

One of the most stressful things when dealing with difficult behaviour is when incidents occur outside the home. Rachel from Sheffield explained how she felt when her son Harrison, aged nine, had a temper tantrum in a local store.

'Harrison is a large child and when he decides he is not going to comply, he will use his weight and throw himself to the ground. We were recently in a shop and he did not want to leave – he started to scream and roll around on the floor, right by the crockery. I can deal with his behaviour, I'm used to it. What I found really difficult was that a group of women standing near by were making comments about my poor parenting skills. I wanted to tell them that he has learning difficulties, but he needed all my attention in order to ensure that he didn't hurt himself or damage the goods in the shop. When I reflected on this afterwards, I felt really angry to be judged in this way.'

Many parents have similar stories to tell. Here are some tips that might help you if behaviour outside the home is a big issue for your child:

- Carry business-sized cards in your pocket explaining that your child has a special need. You can then hand these out if necessary.

- Try to remain calm and ignore comments from others.

- Some parents use printed t-shirts for their children which state they have a special need.

Who can help?

Family and friends

It is important that those close to you understand the behaviour difficulties that you are dealing with as you may need some emotional support while trying to help your child change. You also need to make sure that friends and family deal with your child in a consistent manner and reinforce the boundaries that you put in place.

Other parents

It may be useful to join a parent support group. Sometimes it is helpful to listen to other people's experiences and how they overcame the difficulties. These groups can also be an excellent source of moral support.

Health professionals

Your health visitor will be able to offer you some support in dealing with challenging behaviour if your child is under five. Your GP may be able to signpost you to local services who can offer you support with your child's behaviour.

Summing Up

Remain positive about your child and their behaviour. Remember to always be consistent in the way that you manage behaviours and ensure that everybody is dealing with the behaviour in the same way.

If your child has problems with difficult behaviour, here is a quick list so you can check what action to try first:

- [ ] What is the trigger for your child's problem behaviour? Copy out a few ABC charts from this chapter and fill them in.

- [ ] If you can't work out the trigger, get help from someone who can. Ask your GP or health visitor.

- [ ] When you have spotted the trigger, plan a strategy to help your child. Can you use a reward chart, positive praise or time out?

- [ ] Does your child act up outside the home? Read some tips from this chapter to prepare you and help deal with this behaviour.

Chapter Ten

Sleep Issues

Does your child have sleep problems? If so, you are not alone. Children and young people with special educational needs are far more likely to have serious sleep problems than other children. Sleep deprivation makes it hard for your child to concentrate and learn, so it can magnify their difficulties. Improving sleep can also help all the family. This chapter looks at the effect of sleep deprivation on the whole family, common sleep problems and practical solutions.

Sleep deprivation

Sleep deprivation can have a devastating effect on the whole family and is a leading cause of family stress. Parents may be forced to sleep in shifts in order to attend to their unsettled child. Lack of sleep can also lead parents to take medication, such as stimulants or antidepressants, so that they can function during the day. The unsettled child may be placed in the parents' bedroom in an attempt to pacify them during the night, and siblings may be affected if they share a room.

> Natalie's daughter is eight years old now and has severe sleep difficulties. 'I haven't had a proper night's sleep now since April was born over eight years ago. I cat nap in the day to keep myself going. I don't focus on how tired I am because that would be depressing. I'm up at least three times each night and often our day begins at 4am.'

A child who does not sleep may find it difficult to concentrate in school and may fall asleep at times. Challenging behaviour increases when children are tired, and mental, emotional and physical wellbeing may also be affected.

Tackling the problem

In order to deal with your child's sleep difficulty, work out what is causing the problem. Spend some time thinking about your child's sleep pattern and spend a couple of weeks writing down the time they go to bed, how quickly they fall asleep, the times they wake in the night and the times that they get up in the morning. It may show you if your child has a difficulty settling or if they are waking up for a reason.

If you are going to address a sleep difficulty, it is important that all of those involved with the child are consistent in their approach.

'Spend some time thinking about your child's sleep pattern. It may show you if your child has a difficulty settling or if they are waking up for a reason.'

The bedroom environment

Your child's bedroom should be relaxing and the right environment can help encourage sleep. Look at the following areas and see what simple changes you can make:

Is it over-stimulating?

- Decoration is important. While bright colours may look nice, they can be over-stimulating for children.

- It is unhelpful to have a TV or a computer in the bedroom; if they have to stay then they should be covered up at night time.

- The right curtains can make it easier to help your child sleep. Are your child's curtains thick enough to block out light? If not, buy blackout lining from your local haberdashery store to darken the bedroom.

Is the bed comfortable?

- If your child still sleeps in a cot, is this still big enough for them?

- Could the room be too warm? An overly warm room can disturb sleep.

Is the room quiet?

- Noise is another factor that can impact on your child settling.

- Can you reduce the volume of the family TV and other activities while your child settles?

It is important that your child associates bedtime with going to sleep. Bedrooms are full of toys that are far more tempting than a good night's rest. If possible, store the toys out of sight or cover them over at night.

Bedtime routine

A good bedtime routine is an essential starting point for a good night's sleep. Children enjoy routine and it is important that the same events occur at the same time each night. If you don't already have a bedtime routine then make a start during a bedtime when you know that your child is tired but not overtired.

Here are some ideas:

- An hour before you put your child to bed, work with them to quieten their play.
- Turn the TV and computer games off during this hour.
- Activities like jigsaws and colouring are ideal for this time in the evening.
- Incorporate a relaxing bath into this routine.
- Avoid drinks containing stimulants such as cola, chocolate, tea and coffee – try a warm drink of milk instead.

Once your child has their nightclothes on, they should stay upstairs. Some children need visual clues to understand that night time has arrived:

- Encourage your child to help you close the curtains.
- Tell them clearly that it is night time.
- If they understand the concept of time, look at the clock together.

When your child is in bed, you may wish to read them a short story, which should be roughly the same length each night. Give your child hugs and kisses and tell them clearly 'It is bedtime, go to sleep'. A short phrase that is used repetitively at every bedtime and every night waking can be very effective.

If your child finds it difficult to settle and gets out of bed, take them immediately back to bed without speaking to them. Again, clearly state 'It is bedtime, go to sleep'. Make it clear to them that you will not engage with them during the time that they should be asleep. This is known as 'boring them to sleep'.

Night wakenings

If your child is awakening during the night, you need to have a think about causes. There are a number of reasons why children might awaken during the night. These include:

- Bedwetting.
- Fear of the dark.
- Anxiety at separating from you.
- Noise.
- Different conditions to those that they went to sleep with.
- Inability to self settle.
- Medical reasons.

'Children enjoy routine and it is important that the same events occur at the same time each night.'

Bedwetting

If your child is wetting the bed during the night, be prepared so that you can change them as quickly as possible. Ensure that you have spare clothes and bedding ready and avoid talking.

Here are a few simple steps that can help:

- Avoid giving your child juice, squash and fizzy drinks – blackcurrant juice is known to increase urine output and aggravate night time wetting.
- Encourage your child to empty their bladder at regular intervals throughout the day.
- Encourage them to use the toilet immediately before going to bed.
- Bedwetting alarms can be purchased to awaken your child and avoid accidents.

In the UK, over half a million children between the ages of five and 16 regularly wet the bed. If your child still wets the bed after the age of six, think about consulting your doctor who can arrange to have your child's urine tested for infection.

Fear of the dark

Children may go to sleep with a light shining into their room and awaken to find themselves in complete darkness. They may be confused about this change in conditions. Deal with this fear by:

- Giving your child a touch lamp or torch at the side of their bed.
- Sharing stories with your child that feature characters who are afraid of the dark.

Inability to self settle

We all wake up several times each night, although we may not be aware of waking. Infants generally learn to self settle, but some children do need to be taught this skill. One of the factors stopping children from settling can be a change in conditions. Imagine if you went to sleep in your nice, comfortable bed and woke up to find yourself in a completely different room, how confused would you be? Children who go to sleep with their parents by their side may wake during the night and become distressed because they are alone. The key to resolving this issue is to encourage children to self settle during the bedtime routine. If you have got into the habit of staying with your child while they fall asleep, try gradually moving away from the bed each night. You could start by sitting beside their bed, then in the middle of the room or by the door, before moving to sitting just outside or on the stairs.

If your child does become distressed then re-enter the room and use the bedtime phrase that you have chosen before leaving them to self settle. If you are very anxious about leaving them, you could invest in a wireless CCTV system so that you can see what your child is doing from another room.

The midnight wanderer

Many children get out of bed at night to visit their parents. Getting into the parents' bed is a huge reward for most children and a very difficult problem to resolve once the practice has been established.

If you want to stop your child sleeping in your bed, each time your child enters your room you must automatically take them back to their own bed. A stair gate on your bedroom door may be enough to deter the youngster and encourage them back to bed.

Your child may be distressed, so ensure that they have their comforter when you put them back to bed. If you are so tired that you don't hear your child enter your bedroom then place something near your door that will make a noise once it is opened; for example, wind chimes. Whilst the child joining you may not appear a problem, you may not want to share your bed indefinitely.

Early morning waking

Early morning wakers may wake up at an antisocial hour for a number of reasons. Firstly, it may be that they have genuinely had enough sleep, so if the child isn't showing signs of tiredness during the day, you may need to look at moving their bedtime to a later slot. It may be an environmental factor. Is the light starting to come into the room? Is traffic beginning to create noise outside?

As a family you need to decide what is an acceptable time for your day to begin. Any attempts by your child prior to that time should be treated as a night waking and dealt with as such.

It is important that you help your child's body clock by encouraging them to wake at the same time each day. Some families use a 'good morning' song which they play to waken the child who has no concept of time.

'It is important that you help your child's body clock by encouraging them to wake at the same time each day. Some families use a "good morning" song which they play to waken the child who has no concept of time.'

Medical matters

Some children with special educational needs require medication during the night. Talk to your child's paediatrician about adjusting the routine so it causes as little disturbance as possible for you and your child. If your paediatrician isn't able to offer you alternatives to administering drugs during the bedtime hours, it is important that you are organised at this time. Your aim should be to give the medication with as little interaction with your child as possible so that they can quickly return to sleep.

Epilepsy can be mistaken for a sleep disorder and vice versa. Epilepsy treatment can also affect sleep patterns in children.

Melatonin is a drug that can be used for children with sleep disorders. It is effective for children with visual impairments whose circadian rhythm is disordered. Consultants will want to be sure that you have tried other methods of encouraging your child to sleep prior to prescribing this.

For further information on sleep issues, see *Insomnia – The Essential Guide* (Need2Know).

Who can help?

Family and friends

A supportive network can help you tackle a sleep problem. Ask for support from those close around you and ask people to deal with your child in a consistent manner. When tackling a sleep disorder, the problem may get worse before it gets better – but it is important that you stick with your plan to tackle it. Explain to your friends and family what you are doing and why, and see if they can offer you any additional support over the next couple of weeks. They may be able to look after your child for a couple of hours while you catch up on some sleep, or offer you some company during the evening while you are implementing the bedtime routine.

Other parents

Speaking to parents in a similar situation can be useful. They often have excellent tips and it can leave you feeling less isolated knowing that you aren't the only one struggling at night time.

Health visitors

Your health visitor will be able to offer you support and advice around bedtime routines and how to manage sleep problems effectively.

GP

Your doctor can review your child's medication to see if it could be adding to the sleep difficulties. They will be able to tell you about local agencies who offer support with issues, such as bedwetting and behaviour management, or refer you to a sleep counsellor.

Sleep counsellors

Sleep counsellors are trained workers who support families of children with sleep disorders. They can implement sleep programmes alongside the family in order to improve sleep patterns.

Summing Up

Sleepless nights can bring any parent to their knees. Find out what is causing your child's problems and work through the solutions. Don't forget to ask for help so you can keep going!

Here is a quick list so you can check what action to try next:

☐ Check your child's bedroom. Is it calming and relaxing? If not, cover up toys or move TVs and computers.

☐ Have you got a calming bedtime routine for your child? If not, make plans to play calming games, have a quiet bath and story in the hour before bed.

☐ Is your child waking in the night? Work through the section in this chapter on night waking to find a cause.

☐ Get some help and support for yourself. Start by talking to your health visitor or GP.

☐ Sleep Scotland is a charity that supports parents and carers of children and young people with additional support needs and sleep problems. You will find information on how to contact them in the help list at the end of this book.

Chapter Eleven

Education

The education system can seem like a minefield when your child has a special educational need. This chapter looks at how the system works and where you can find support to get your child an education to meet their needs.

The early years

It is important that your child has access to pre-school activities to support their development. Many parents think that their child is unable to go to play groups and pre-schools if they have a special need; however, all children have a right to early years education. You can choose from private day nurseries, playgroups, Sure Start centres and childminders. Your local council's early years and childcare provision team will be able to give you information on local options for your child.

When choosing a setting, you may wish to consider the following:

- Are the staff experienced at dealing with children with special needs? If your child uses Makaton, for example, can staff sign?
- Is the environment stimulating and pleasant?
- Is the environment easy for your child to move around?

Write your own thoughts about the ideal place for your child:......................
....
....
....

Ask for a meeting with the centre's SENCO so you can discuss your child's needs in full.

Early Years Action

Once your child is in a setting, they may be given special help with their learning, which is called Early Years Action. It may mean teaching your child in a different way or providing them with additional adult support. The SENCO may use an Individual Education Plan (IEP). See later on in this chapter for a full explanation of an IEP.

Early Years Action Plus

Early Years Action Plus is used when staff identify that additional help is needed from an outside specialist, for example a speech therapist. Specialists who are external to the setting may make an assessment of what is needed and advise on the IEP, or they may spend time working directly with your child.

The Portage Service

The Portage Service is a home visiting service for pre-school children with additional needs. It aims to support your child in developing play, communication and relationship skills. It can also help you become more confident in developing your child. Ask your health visitor if a Portage service operates locally or visit the Portage website at www.portage.org.uk.

Who can help?

SENCO – a member of staff who has responsibility for overseeing the children with special educational needs in the setting. They will ensure that your child receives the correct level of support.

School age children

If your child's teacher has concerns about their development, they will be given additional support called School Action. This may involve a different way of teaching, additional help or use of particular equipment. You should be consulted at each stage about your child's progress and an Individual Education Plan may also be used. If your child does not make enough progress, the school may then talk to you about asking advice from other specialists from outside the school. This kind of help is known as School Action Plus. If the school cannot give your child the help that they need then it may be necessary to ask for a statutory assessment for your child.

The Special Educational Needs Code of Practice

The SEN Code of Practice is a document that gives guidance to schools and the LA to help identify, assess and support children with additional needs. Processes and procedures that schools have to go through are set out in this document. You can request a free copy of this from the Department of Education (see help list) if you would like to have a reference copy.

Statutory assessment

If your child needs a great deal of help or extra resources, the LA may decide to make a statutory assessment. It is carried out by your LA and they will ask specialists for advice about your child. It is unusual for children under two to be assessed for a statement.

You can ask in writing for an assessment for your child. The ACE centre (see help list) produces a template letter for parents to use. Your child's school or nursery can also request an assessment but must speak to you before doing so.

Statement of Special Educational Needs

A statement sets out your child's needs and ensures that they receive the support that they need. A statement is set out in six sections:

- Section 1 gives information about your child.

- Section 2 describes your child's needs following the assessment.

- Section 3 outlines the special help to be given to your child.

- Section 4 names the school and type of provision your child should attend.

- Section 5 describes any non-educational needs that your child has.

- Section 6 outlines how your child will get help to meet any non-educational needs.

You will be sent a draft copy of the statement before the LA writes the final version. Section 4 will be left blank for you to state what educational provision you want for your child. You have 15 days to comment on the statement and you may disagree with all or part of it. You may also ask to meet with the LA. They must complete the final statement within eight weeks of issuing the draft statement.

Disagreeing with statements

If you don't agree with the statement you must:

- First speak to your 'named officer'. You will be given their details at the beginning of the process.

- You may also wish to speak to your local Parent Partnership Service (see later on in this chapter).

- Consider appealing to the Special Educational Needs and Disability Tribunal (SENDIST). Your LA will inform you of local arrangements.

Individual Education Plans

Individual Education Plans (IEPs) are used to plan and review your child's learning. They state what specialist help is being given to your child, how this is provided and how often. The plan sets out small, achievable targets for your child. It is reviewed regularly and you should be encouraged to work with staff to help your child towards the goals.

Annual reviews

The statement is reviewed once a year to make sure that it remains accurate and that the support given meets your child's needs. Before the meeting you will be invited to send in your views on your child's progress over the last 12 months. You will be asked to attend the review meeting, together with the professionals involved with your child. The meeting will look at written reports and your child's statement. Any changes are agreed and sent to the LA within 10 days of the meeting. They may then decide to update the statement.

Parent Partnership Service

Parent Partnership Services offer impartial information, advice and support to parents of children with special educational needs. They are able to put you in contact with other local organisations and work hard to make sure that your views are heard.

Choosing a school

Deciding which school to send your child to can be difficult. Visit several schools to help you consider what sort of setting is the right one for your child and ask to speak to staff and other parents to get a good idea of how the school operates.

Mainstream schools

Most children with special educational needs are taught in mainstream school. Some schools have specialist units attached to them where children can gain additional support yet be integrated with their peers. Contact your LA to find out what units are available in your area and whether these may meet your child's needs.

Special schools

Mainstream schools are able to cater for the majority of children's needs. Special schools only take children with particular special educational needs and may cater for children from the age of two up to 19. Contact your local council's special needs department for information about the special schools in your area and what needs they cater for. Children need a Statement of Special Educational Needs to attend a special school.

You may also wish to consider non-maintained special schools, which are usually run by charities, independent special schools or schools maintained by a neighbouring LA. However, if there is a suitable local state school, your LA does not have to provide funding for your preferred school.

Pupil Referral Units

Pupil Referral Units (PRUs) provide education to children of compulsory school age who because of illness, exclusion or other issues are unable to attend a school in the LA. The number of pupils in a PRU varies, as does the pattern of attendance for each child. Children usually attend a PRU for a fixed time and are then reintegrated into their previous school or moved on to a different school.

Home education

Home tutors employed by the LA visit your child at home to teach them, but they are only used in exceptional circumstances. You can choose to educate your child at home; in fact many parents of children with special needs have moved to home education. Whether a child has a statement of special educational needs or not, permission is not needed to withdraw a child from a mainstream school in order to begin home education. Your child may be withdrawn from school in the normal way by sending a letter to the head teacher to inform the school that you will be home educating your child. If, however, your child attends a special school or unit, you would need to ask for the head teacher's consent in your letter.

Further information about home education can be found at the Home Education Advisory Service, www.heas.org.uk.

Summing Up

You are the expert on your child. Wherever you choose for their education, you should be included in every step of the decision making process. Talk with staff regularly and if you have concerns about your child's education, raise them immediately.

Here is a quick checklist so you can check what action to try next:

☐ Develop good relationships with your child's educational providers.

☐ Go in and look round before accepting a place.

☐ Make use of the support services that are available to ensure you are well informed and empowered when making decisions about educational matters.

Chapter Twelve

Housing and Finance

It can cost up to three times more to bring up a child with a disability, so it is no wonder that many families struggle to cope financially. This chapter looks at the help that you may be able to get. It will also look at the issue of housing and help if you need to make alterations to accommodate your child.

Financial pressure on families

Most people have some debt in their lives, but families where the child has an additional need may face more financial hardship than others.

'When I had Simon, I was only supposed to be having a few months off work. As it turned out, his needs meant that he needed full-time care and the option of me returning to work was ruled out. This meant that we were living on a fraction of the income that we had planned. Added to that, we had to do lots of trips to the hospital, so the petrol costs mounted up and so did the parking costs.'

Many families are forced to live on one wage with one parent becoming the carer for their child. Other parents face the costs of transporting their child to hospital on a regular basis, additional bedding, specialist equipment – the list goes on!

'Most people have some debt in their lives, but families where the child has an additional need may face more financial hardship than others.'

Debt

If you are in debt, make a list of exactly what you owe to whom. Then look at which debts are priorities, like your mortgage and utility bills. Non-priority debts may include store cards, credit cards and loans that are not secured against your home. Switch debts with the highest rate of interest to a lower rate if possible and keep paying as much as you can to clear your debts quickly.

Speak to your creditors to alert them of your difficulties. Contact your local Citizen's Advice to get help with this and working out a plan to beat your debt, or call the National Debtline on 0808 808 4000 for support from a trained advisor to help you reduce your debts significantly.

Increase your income

Think about some ideas to increase the amount of money that comes into your home each month:

- Selling goods on auction websites or going to a car boot sale can help you to declutter the house and make some cash. Children's second-hand clothing sells particularly well when you sell a number of items in a bundle.

- Working overtime can give your finances a boost, but it may reduce the amount of benefit that you can claim. An advisor at Contact a Family will be able to help you with this.

- Taking in a lodger, if your home is large enough.

- Starting a home business. Identify a skill that you have and become self-employed. If you have office skills, you could type for local companies. Maybe you are crafty and could make handmade greetings cards. This will allow you the flexibility of working around your child's needs. Register as self-employed with the Inland Revenue within three months of starting.

- Becoming a mystery shopper. Agencies pay you to visit local stores and restaurants and file a report. Search on the Internet for details of reputable companies.

Benefits

You may be entitled to benefits and tax credits that you aren't claiming. Make a regular benefit check to find out if you can claim any extra. You can call the Contact a Family helpline on 0808 808 3555 (Mon to Fri, 10am-4pm, Mon, 5.30-7.30pm) to see if you are missing out on anything. You can also get information on benefits from your local Jobcentre Plus.

Funds to consider

As well as benefits, there are a number of funds that you may consider applying to for additional help.

The Family Fund

The Family Fund awards lump sums to families for items to support the care of a child who is 17 or under with a severe disability or illness. Ask for funding to help with things such as clothing, transport expenses, holidays and white goods. Your financial circumstances will be taken into account. To get the application form, telephone 0845 130 4542 or email info@familyfund.org.uk.

> 'I have just received money from the Family Fund to make my garden area safe. It is going to be fantastic for my little girl this summer. It will be the first time that she will be able to play out in the garden, I'm so glad that I applied.' June, mum to a three-year-old.

Social care

Social care can offer families additional financial support in exceptional circumstances. If you are in a difficult situation and face eviction or having your power supply cut off, it may be worth contacting your local social care department.

Education Maintenance Allowance

This is for families that have a 16- or 17-year-old still in education. Your child's school or college should be able to give you details about making a claim. Receiving this allowance will not affect your other benefits.

Individual charities

If your child has a specific diagnosis, it may be worth researching the charities involved in this area as some may offer grants for individuals.

Directory of Social Change

This organisation publishes a book called *A Guide to Grants for Individuals in Need*. It contains information on national and local charities that contribute to individuals in need. Ask at your local library.

Getting the right equipment

The right equipment in your home can make life far easier. Social care should provide necessary equipment for everyday living and non-medical needs, and the health authority should provide you with equipment for medical or nursing needs.

Contact your GP or social worker and explain what equipment you would like or the problem that you have. They will arrange a home visit for an occupational therapist to assess your child. The occupational therapist will advise you on what equipment will help and may work with a nursing professional if the equipment is for medical needs.

Making your home safe

It is vital that your child is safe in your home. If you have concerns about any aspect of your home's safety, discuss this with the occupational therapist. They are able to assess the home and provide devices to make it safer.

'My daughter had a habit of opening the windows upstairs – I was terrified that she would fall out. I spoke to the occupational therapist about my worries and she was able to provide window catches, which means that the windows now only open slightly. It is good not to have that constant fear and was so simple to resolve'. Jonathan, Birmingham.

Housing adaptations

It may be that your home needs to be adapted if your child has a physical disability. The Disabled Facilities Grant can help with the cost of adaptations. The work that you are applying to have done must be approved as being 'necessary and appropriate' in meeting your child's needs. For the most up-to-date information, call Contact a Family on 0808 808 3555.

LAs provide financial and other assistance for improvements or repairs to the home. Contact your local housing authority to find out how they may be able to assist. Application forms are available from the local housing or environmental health department. They will not fund work that has already been started or completed.

'It is vital that your child is safe in your home. If you have concerns about any aspect of your home's safety, discuss this with the occupational therapist. They are able to assess the home and provide devices to make it safer.'

Summing Up

Family finances can be stretched to the limit by extra costs and it can be hard to find your way out of debt. However, there are organisations to help you. You may also be able to get help with the costs of essential adaptations to your home.

Here is a quick checklist of actions to try next:

- [ ] Take a benefit check to make sure you are claiming what you are entitled to.

- [ ] If you are in debt, take some positive action and contact an advisor to begin to plan your way out of debt.

- [ ] Assess your home for safety and speak to an occupational therapist about equipment that may help.

Help List

Speech

Afasic

1st Floor, 20 Bowling Green Lane, London, EC1R 0BD
Tel: 0845 3 55 55 77 (helpline)
www.afasic.org.uk
www.afasiccymru.org.uk
www.afasicnorthernireland.org.uk
www.afasicscotland.org.uk
Helps children and young people affected by the hidden disability of speech, language and communication impairments, their families and the professionals working with them. You can email enquiries through their website.

The Association of Speech and Language Therapists in Independent Practice (ASLTIP)

Coleheath Bottom, Speen, Princes Risborough, Bucks, HP27 0SZ
Tel: 01494 488306
www.helpwithtalking.com
Provides information on independent speech and language therapy.

I CAN

8 Wakley Street, London, EC1V 7QE
Tel: 0845 225 4073 (information)
info@ican.org.uk
www.ican.org.uk
Working alongside children with speech, language and communication needs. I CAN also work with families and train and support Early Year's staff, teachers and speech and language therapists (SLTs). I CAN provides www.talkingpoint.org.uk, a site for information about communication development and disability.

Global developmental delay

Making Contact

www.makingcontact.org
An organisation that puts parents in touch with each other.

Mumszone

www.mumszone.co.uk
This website has a special needs forum where you can chat to other parents in similar positions – dads are welcome too.

Parents centre

www.direct.gov.uk
Click on 'parents.' This is a resource to support parents, with information covering issues such as money, childcare, schools and development.

Autistic spectrum disorder

The Asperger's Syndrome Foundation

Finsbury Square Charity Centre, Royal London House, Suite 5A,1st Floor, 22-25 Finsbury Square, London, EC2A 1DX
info@aspergerfoundation.org.uk
www.aspergerfoundation.org.uk
A charity committed to promoting awareness and understanding of Asperger's syndrome.

The National Autistic Society

Tel: 0845 070 4004 (helpline)
www.nas.org.uk
Championing the rights and interests of all people with autism.
Useful resources for parents including an online shop where specialist resources can be purchased. National and regional contacts can be found on the website.

Pyramid Educational Consultants

Pavilion House, 6 Old Steine, Brighton, BN1 1EJ
Tel: 01273 609555
pyramiduk@pecs.com
www.pecs.org.uk
Sells PECS (Picture Exchange Communication Systems), a communication system where children are able to select pictures of familiar items and hand them to you to make their needs known. For example, if a child would like a drink of milk, they will find the picture of the glass of milk and hand it to the adult. The adult will then exchange the picture for a glass of milk.

Hearing and Sight

The British Association of Behavioural Optometrists

21 Hartlebury Way, Charlton Kings, Cheltenham, Gloucestershire, GL52 6YB
Tel: 01242 575107
admin@babo.co.uk
www.babo.co.uk
Find optometrists with a special interest in improving your child's visual function.

Deafness Research UK Information Service

330-332 Gray's Inn Road, London, WC1X 8EE
Tel: 0808 808 2222 (information service)
info@deafnessresearch.org.uk
www.deafnessresearch.org.uk
A medical charity for deaf and hard of hearing people. Contact for information on hearing loss and its causes.

Early Support

www.earlysupport.org.uk
For families with children aged five years and under with additional needs.
Early Support was developed by parents, carers and practitioners.

Look Up Information

SeeAbility House, Hook Road, Epsom, Surrey, KT19 8SQ
Tel: 01372 755 066 (information)
info@lookupinfo.org
www.lookupinfo.org
Information about eye care and vision for people with learning difficulties.

National Deaf Children's Society

15 Dufferin Street, London, EC1Y 8UR
Tel: 0808 800 8880 (helpline)
helpline@ndcs.org.uk
www.ndcs.org.uk
Provides a wide range of information and advice about childhood deafness, family support and equipment.

Physical disability

Contact a Family

209-211 City Road, London, EC1V 1JN
Tel: 0808 808 3555 (helpline)
helpline@cafamily.org.uk
www.cafamily.org.uk
Provides advice, information and support to parents of disabled children – no matter what their disability or health condition is. The charity also enables parents to get in contact with other families on a local and national basis.

Direct.gov

www.direct.gov.uk
Provides current information about health, education, benefits and many more services offered by local and national government.

Whizz-Kidz

Elliot House, 10-12 Allington Street, London, SW1E 5EH
www.whizz-kidz.org.uk

Whizz-Kidz gives disabled children the chance to lead a more independent life. The charity offers advice, training and assessment for mobility equipment.

Genetic and hereditary conditions

The Down's Syndrome Association

Langdon Down Centre, 2a Langdon Park, Teddington, TW11 9PS
Tel: 0845 230 0372 (helpline)
info@downs-syndrome.org.uk
www.downs-syndrome.org.uk
Helping people with Down's syndrome to live full and rewarding lives.

The Fragile X Society

Rood End House, 6 Stortford Road, Great Dunmow, Essex, CM6 1DA
Tel: 01371 875100
info@fragilex.org.uk
www.fragilex.org.uk
Provides support, information and friendship for families whose children and relatives have Fragile X syndrome.

Home-Start UK

8-10 West Walk, Leicester, Leicestershire, LE1 7NA
Tel: 0800 068 6368
www.home-start.org.uk
Provides help and support if you feel like you are struggling. Home-Start supplies volunteers to give you a break, a listening ear and an extra pair of hands. Local groups can be found online.

Joseph Patrick Trust

Tel: 020 7803 4814
www.muscular-dystrophy.org
Provides equipment grants for people with muscular dystrophy. Click on 'how we help you' and then 'equipment grants.'

Muscular Dystrophy Campaign

61 Southwark Street, London, SE1 0HL
Tel: 0800 652 6352
info@muscular-dystrophy.org
www.muscular-dystrophy.org
Supporting families and those with muscular dystrophy.

The Snowdon Award Scheme

Unit 18, Oakhurst Business Park, Wilberforce Way, Southwater, RH13 9RT
Tel: 01403 732899
info@snowdonawardscheme.org.uk
www.snowdonawardscheme.org.uk
Provides grants towards disability-related expenses for young adults in higher or further education.

S.O.F.T UK (Support Organisation For Trisomy 13/18 and Related Disorders)

Tel: 0121 351 3122
www.soft.org.uk
For families affected by trisomy 13/18 and related disorders, and rare conditions for whom no other organisation exists. You can email enquiries through the website. Contact details for Scotland and Northern Ireland can be found on the website.

Specific learning difficulties

The British Dyslexia Association

Unit 8, Bracknell Beeches, Old Bracknell Lane, Bracknell, RG12 7BW
Tel: 0845 251 9002
helpline@bdadyslexia.org.uk
www.bdadyslexia.org.uk
Promotes early identification and support in schools to ensure opportunities to learn for dyslexic learners.

The Dyspraxia Foundation

8 West Alley, Hitchin, Herts, SG5 1EG
Tel: 01462 454 986 (helpline)
dyspraxia@dyspraxiafoundation.org.uk
www.dyspraxiafoundation.org.uk
This organisation can put you in touch with local groups, answer your questions or send you information.

Netmums

www.netmums.com
Has a special needs forum where you can post messages and hear from other parents.

Family life

Contact a Family

209-211 City Road, London, EC1V 1JN
Tel: 0808 808 3555 (helpline)
helpline@cafamily.org.uk
www.cafamily.org.uk
Produces a factsheet about grandparenting a child with special needs. Copies can be downloaded from the website.

Face 2 Face

Tel: 0844 800 9189
face2facenetwork@scope.org.uk
www.face2facenetwork.org.uk
A national befriending service where parents are trained to befriend other parents online, by telephone or, if there is a scheme in your area, face to face. Log onto their website to find out where the schemes are located and how to take part.

Home-Start

8-10 West Walk, Leicester, Leicestershire, LE1 7NA
Tel: 0800 068 6368

www.home-start.org.uk
A national organisation that can offer support to families that are struggling to cope simply due to a new baby, lack of family nearby, death or illness.

Sibs

Meadowfield, Oxenhope, West Yorkshire, BD22 9JD
Tel: 01535 645 453
www.sibs.org.uk
Provides sibling support for people who have a disabled brother or sister.

Special Kids in the UK

www.specialkidsintheuk.org
A website set up by parents to support parents. Includes an online forum which is a great place to share information and gain support.

Behaviour

NSPCC

NSPCC Helpline, 42 Curtain Road, London, EC2A 3NH
Tel: 0808 800 5000 (help and advice)
www.nspcc.org.uk
Produces a number of leaflets around behaviour management and positive parenting. These can be downloaded from the website for a small charge.

Oaasis

The Croft, Vicars Hill, Boldre, Lymington, Hants, SO41 5QB
Tel: 0800 197 3907 (helpline)
oaasis@cambiangroup.com
www.oaasis.co.uk
Produces a range of 'What is?' cards which are free to download. They explain simply why your child may be behaving inappropriately and are ideal to hand out if your child's behaviour is challenging while out and about.

Up and Down Charts

18 Laurels Road, Offenham, Evesham, Worcestershire, WR11 8RE

www.upanddowncharts.co.uk
Produces magnetic reward charts that are easy to use to reward your child's good behaviour.

The Webster-Stratton Parenting Course

Looks at dealing with challenging behaviours in younger children. Ask your health visitor or local children's centre about any courses running in your area.

Sleep

Cerebra

Second Floor Offices, Lyric Buildings, King Street, Carmarthen, SA31 1BD
Tel: 0800 328 1159 (parent support helpline)
www.cerebra.org.uk
An organisation supporting brain injured children and young people. Their sleep counsellor is available to offer support.

Contact a Family

209-211 City Road, London, EC1V 1JN
Tel: 0808 808 3555 (helpline)
info@cafamily.org.uk
www.cafamily.org.uk
Produces a series of useful leaflets for parents, including one about sleep difficulties. Visit the website to download.

ERIC

34 Old School House, Britannia Road, Kingswood, Bristol, BS15 8DB
Tel: 0845 370 8008
www.eric.org.uk
Provides information and support for children, young people and parents on bedwetting, daytime wetting and soiling. Items such as bedding protection and alarms can be purchased online.

Lynn Wilshaw

Tel: 01709 875475

www.tickhillcounselling.co.uk
Offers a sleep counselling service for children and families.

Sleep Scotland

Tel: 0131 651 1392 (support line)
www.sleepscotland.org
This organisation supports families of children with additional needs who have severe sleep problems throughout Scotland. It trains and supports sleep counsellors. Free information leaflets can be downloaded from the website.

Sleep Solutions

Tel: 01432 355808
sleepsolutions@scope.org.uk
Supported by Scope and in partnership with Sleep Scotland, this service supports families across England with sleep management difficulties by providing workshops facilitated by trained sleep counsellors.

Education

Advisory Centre for Education (Ace)

1c Aberdeen Studios, 22 Highbury Grove, London, N5 2DQ
Tel: 0808 800 5793
www.ace-ed.org.uk
Provides information about state education in England and Wales for children aged five to 16, with telephone advice on special educational needs matters.

Department for Education

www.education.gov.uk
Responsible for education and children's services.

Home Education Advisory Service

Tel: 01707 371854
www.heas.org.uk

The national home education charity. HEAS is dedicated to providing parents with advice and support for educating their children at home. HEAS offers information for home educators including advice about educational materials, resources, GCSE examinations, special educational needs, information technology, legal matters and curriculum design. HEAS produces a range of leaflets and the *Home Education Handbook*.

Independent Panel for Special Education Advice (IPSEA)

Hunters Court, Debden Road, Saffron Walden, CB11 4AA
Tel: 0800 018 4016 (advice line)
www.ipsea.org.uk
Independent experts who will give you free advice about your child's special educational needs.

Parents for Inclusion

Tel: 0800 652 3145 (helpline)
info@parentsforinclusion.org
www.parentsforinclusion.org
Helping disabled children to learn, make friends and have a voice in school.

Parent Partnership Service

Council for Disabled Children, 8 Wakley Street, London, EC1V 7QE
Tel: 0207 843 6058
www.parentpartnership.org.uk
Provides impartial advice and support around special educational needs issues. You can search for your local services here.

Finance

Abilitynet

Tel: 0800 269545
enquiries@abilitynet.org.uk
www.abilitynet.co.uk
Offers advice on computers and software for children with a disability. They can advise on financial assistance from charitable trusts for equipment.

Disabled Living Foundation

380-384 Harrow Road, London, W9 2HU
Tel: 0845 130 9177 (helpline)
info@dlf.org.uk
www.dlf.org.uk
Produces factsheets about children's daily living equipment. These can be downloaded from their website or you can call the helpline.

Family Fund

4 Alpha Court, Monks Cross Drive, York, YO32 9WN
Tel: 0845 130 4542
info@familyfund.org.uk
www.familyfund.org.uk
The Family Fund helps families with severely disabled children to have choices and the opportunity to enjoy ordinary life. Contact the organisation for grants and funding information.

Need – 2 – Know

Need - 2 - Know

Available Titles Include ...

Allergies A Parent's Guide
ISBN 978-1-86144-064-8 £8.99

Autism A Parent's Guide
ISBN 978-1-86144-069-3 £8.99

Drugs A Parent's Guide
ISBN 978-1-86144-043-3 £8.99

Dyslexia and Other Learning Difficulties
A Parent's Guide ISBN 978-1-86144-042-6 £8.99

Bullying A Parent's Guide
ISBN 978-1-86144-044-0 £8.99

Epilepsy The Essential Guide
ISBN 978-1-86144-063-1 £8.99

Teenage Pregnancy The Essential Guide
ISBN 978-1-86144-046-4 £8.99

Gap Years The Essential Guide
ISBN 978-1-86144-079-2 £8.99

How to Pass Exams A Parent's Guide
ISBN 978-1-86144-047-1 £8.99

Child Obesity A Parent's Guide
ISBN 978-1-86144-049-5 £8.99

Applying to University The Essential Guide
ISBN 978-1-86144-052-5 £8.99

ADHD The Essential Guide
ISBN 978-1-86144-060-0 £8.99

Student Cookbook - Healthy Eating The Essential Guide
ISBN 978-1-86144-061-7 £8.99

Stress The Essential Guide
ISBN 978-1-86144-054-9 £8.99

Adoption and Fostering A Parent's Guide
ISBN 978-1-86144-056-3 £8.99

Special Educational Needs A Parent's Guide
ISBN 978-1-86144-057-0 £8.99

The Pill An Essential Guide
ISBN 978-1-86144-058-7 £8.99

University A Survival Guide
ISBN 978-1-86144-072-3 £8.99

Diabetes The Essential Guide
ISBN 978-1-86144-059-4 £8.99

View the full range at **www.need2knowbooks.co.uk**. To order our titles, call **01733 898103**, email **sales@n2kbooks.com** or visit the website.

Need - 2 - Know, Remus House, Coltsfoot Drive, Peterborough, PE2 9JX